ONE-POT
Wonders
eat well without the washing up

MURDOCH BOOKS

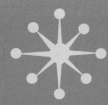

One-pot cooking is the ultimate in no-fuss cuisine. The concept couldn't be easier: all your ingredients are cooked together in the same pan, pot or dish. Your meal just seems to cook itself, filling your kitchen with enticing aromas, and when it's ready it is so easy to serve, with minimal washing-up required afterwards. You'd be surprised how many fabulous dishes you can conjure up in just one pot: all manner of tasty soups, stews, bakes, braises, curries, hotpots, pasta dishes, roasts and risottos, conveniently gathered together here. Some meals beg a simple accompaniment —but a green salad or some chopped avocados are about as demanding as it gets!

Contents

06 *Simmered*

Flavours develop in the most delectable way when they're allowed to bubble and blend on the stovetop. Whether you crave the comfort of soup, pasta or risotto, need to refuel body and soul with a hearty hotpot or yearn to be transported to exotic places via couscous, gumbo or a heady curry, in this chapter you are spoilt for choice.

106 *Baked*

Throw all your ingredients in a baking or casserole dish and let the oven do all the hard work; it almost feels like cheating! But no-one will accuse you of taking shortcuts when these mouthwatering meals make it to the table — whether you want to serve up a classic roast chicken, a rich ricotta, provolone and salami pie, some rustic baked beans or a parcel of fragrant, juicy fish, you'll find them all here.

Simmered

Moroccan honey lamb shanks with root vegetables • Pancetta and blue cheese risotto • Chicken, tomato and okra curry • Spinach dhal • Chicken tagine with dates, lemon and pistachios • Veal and eggplant ragu with pappardelle • Chicken and rice with lemongrass and ginger • Japanese beef and potato stew • Spicy fish couscous • Iranian beef noodle soup • Saffron chicken with fennel and green olive tapénade • Slow-braised spiced beef with prunes and silverbeet • Seafood and sausage gumbo • Cameroon pork curry • Penne with pesto, bocconcini and cherry tomatoes • Mexican meatball soup • Seafood fideus • Spanish pork casserole • Chicken, sausage and corn soup • Beef braciola • Tuscan-style ribollita • Chicken mole • Soba noodle soup with salmon • Prawn and lime pilaff • Osso buco with potatoes and orange olive gremolata • Pork won ton soup • Madrid cocido • Avgolemono with chicken meatballs • Noodle hotpot with beef and tofu • Cambodian-style fish, tomato and pineapple soup • Braised pork belly with daikon and greens • Creamy ricotta ravioli with silverbeet, nutmeg and lemon • Chicken and black bean soup with avocado salsa • Mee goreng • Sweet and sour pork noodle stir-fry • Beef and carrot stew with five-spice and star anise • Chicken risoni with orange and basil • Tofu, cashew and noodle stir-fry • Beef pho • Mussel and sweet corn chowder • Pork and egg pad Thai • Beef borscht • Steamed Cantonese chicken with ginger and snow peas • Chicken liver and mushroom sauté with spinach and cream • Harira • Satay chicken noodles • Pork and noodles in lemongrass broth • Salmon with braised pumpkin and sesame cream • Lamb, lemon and barley soup

Moroccan honey lamb shanks with root vegetables

Instead of lemon zest, you can add a quarter of a preserved lemon, rinsed and thinly sliced. If, by the end of cooking, the sauce is not as thick as you would like, carefully remove the shanks and vegetables to a plate using tongs, then cover and keep them warm while boiling the sauce a little longer until reduced to the desired consistency.

1 tablespoon olive oil
4 frenched lamb shanks (about 1.25 kg/ 2 lb 12 oz in total), trimmed
1 onion, halved and sliced
2 garlic cloves, crushed
2 tablespoons ras el hanout (available from delicatessens), or Moroccan spice mix (available from supermarkets)
500 ml (17 fl oz/2 cups) beef stock
90 g (3¼ oz/¼ cup) honey
60 g (2¼ oz/½ cup) raisins
2 strips lemon zest, each about 2 cm (¾ inch) wide, all white pith removed
1 parsnip
1 large carrot
250 g (9 oz) sweet potato
155 g (5½ oz/1 cup) fresh or frozen green peas
toasted slivered almonds, to serve
1 small handful flat-leaf (Italian) parsley, roughly chopped

Heat the olive oil in a large flameproof casserole dish or heavy-based saucepan. Add the shanks, in batches if necessary, and cook, turning often, for 5 minutes, or until browned all over. Remove to a plate.

Add the onion and garlic to the casserole dish and sauté for 5 minutes, or until the onion has softened. Stir in the spice mix and cook for 1 minute, or until aromatic, then add the stock, honey, raisins and lemon zest and stir to combine. Bring to the boil, then add the shanks and reduce the heat to low. Cover and simmer for 1 hour, turning the shanks once.

Peel the parsnip, carrot and sweet potato and cut into 4 cm (1½ inch) chunks. Add the vegetables to the casserole, pushing them down to cover them in the liquid, then cover and cook for a further 30 minutes. Skim off any excess fat, increase the heat to medium and cook for 20–30 minutes, uncovered, until the vegetables and meat are nearly tender. Add the peas and cook for another 10 minutes; the liquid should have reduced and thickened a little and the meat and vegetables should be very tender. Remove the lemon zest.

Divide the shanks among warm serving plates. Spoon the sauce and vegetables over the shanks, scatter with the almonds and parsley and serve.

Preparation time: 20 minutes   **Cooking time:** 2 hours 30 minutes   **Serves:** 4

✳ **Preparation time:** 20 minutes   ✳ **Cooking time:** 40 minutes   ✳ **Serves:** 4

Pancetta and blue cheese risotto

1½ tablespoons olive oil
175 g (6 oz) piece of pancetta,
  finely chopped
¼ cabbage (about 400 g/14 oz),
  core and outer leaves removed,
  then thinly sliced
1 onion, finely chopped
1 garlic clove, crushed
300 g (10½ oz/1⅓ cups) arborio rice
125 ml (4 fl oz/½ cup) white wine
1 litre (35 fl oz/4 cups) hot chicken
  or vegetable stock, approximately
20 g (¾ oz) butter
50 g (1¾ oz) mild blue cheese,
  crumbled
1 small handful flat-leaf (Italian)
  parsley, chopped

Heat half the olive oil in a large heavy-based saucepan over medium heat. Add the pancetta and sauté for 4 minutes, or until light golden, then add the cabbage and sauté for another 4–5 minutes, or until the cabbage has wilted. Remove the mixture to a bowl and set aside.

Heat the remaining oil in the pan. Add the onion and garlic and sauté for 5 minutes, or until the onion is softened but not browned. Add the rice and stir to coat the grains in the oil, then stir in the wine and allow to simmer until almost all the liquid has evaporated. Pour in 125 ml (4 fl oz/½ cup) of the hot stock and continue cooking, stirring often, until the liquid has been almost absorbed.

Add another 125 ml (4 fl oz/½ cup) of the hot stock and cook, stirring often, until almost absorbed. Continue stirring the rice and adding the stock for a further 10–12 minutes, or until the stock has mostly all been absorbed and the rice is al dente. It may be necessary to add a little more stock or water — the risotto should be creamy and will take about 20 minutes to cook.

Stir in the butter, blue cheese, the cabbage mixture and half the parsley. Divide the risotto among warm bowls and serve sprinkled with the remaining parsley.

Add more blue cheese if desired — the actual amount will depend on the taste and depth of flavour of the individual cheese. If pancetta is not available, use bacon instead.

Native to west Africa, okra is a vegetable from the marrow family, along with cocoa and cotton. Avoid buying specimens that are too large as these have little flavour — select ones around 10 cm (4 inches) long, with an even green colour. They should be firm when gently pressed. If okra is soft or has blotchy skin it is past its prime.

Chicken, tomato and okra curry

60 g (2¼ oz/¼ cup) Madras curry paste
2 garlic cloves, finely chopped
2 teaspoons grated fresh ginger
1 teaspoon fennel seeds
4 chicken leg quarters (marylands),
   about 1.25 kg (2 lb 12 oz in total),
   cut in half through the joint
20 g (¾ oz) butter
1 tablespoon vegetable oil
1 onion, chopped
1 green chilli, seeded and chopped
1 cinnamon stick
4 green cardamom pods, crushed
400 g (14 oz) tin chopped tomatoes
200 g (7 oz) okra, trimmed and sliced
warm naan bread, to serve

Put the curry paste, garlic, ginger and fennel seeds in a small food processor and blend until a paste forms. Remove the spice paste to a large bowl, add the chicken pieces and toss well to coat. Season with sea salt and freshly ground black pepper and set aside.

Heat the butter and oil in a large heavy-based saucepan. Add the onion and chilli and sauté over medium–low heat for 3–5 minutes, or until the onion has softened. Add the chicken pieces in batches and cook for 5–6 minutes, turning often, until browned all over. Return all the chicken to the pan and add the cinnamon stick, cardamom, tomatoes and 125 ml (4 fl oz/½ cup) water. Bring the mixture to a simmer, then cover and cook over low heat for 15 minutes.

Mix the okra through and cook, uncovered, for another 30 minutes, or until the chicken and okra are tender. Serve with warm naan bread.

✳ **Preparation time:** 20 minutes   ✳ **Cooking time:** 1 hour   ✳ **Serves:** 4–6

Preparation time: 15 minutes   **Cooking time:** 1 hour 10 minutes   **Serves:** 4

Spinach dhal

1½ tablespoons vegetable oil
1 onion, finely chopped
1 garlic clove, crushed
½ teaspoon ground turmeric
½ teaspoon chilli powder
1 teaspoon cumin seeds
1 teaspoon mustard seeds
330 g (11½ oz/1½ cups) yellow split
  peas, rinsed and drained
250 g (9 oz) packet frozen spinach,
  thawed, then squeezed as dry as
  possible
1 small handful coriander (cilantro)
  leaves, chopped
2 teaspoons garam masala
1½ tablespoons lemon juice
mango chutney, to serve
Greek-style yoghurt, to serve
warm naan bread, to serve

Heat the oil in a flameproof casserole dish over medium heat. Add the onion and sauté for 5 minutes, or until softened. Add the garlic, turmeric, chilli powder, cumin seeds and mustard seeds and stir for a further 2 minutes, or until the spices are fragrant and the mustard seeds start to pop.

Add the split peas and 875 ml (30 fl oz/ 3½ cups) cold water. Bring to the boil, then cover and simmer, stirring occasionally, for 50–60 minutes, or until the split peas are tender and the liquid is almost absorbed.

Remove the dhal from the heat, then stir in the spinach, coriander, garam masala and lemon juice. Season to taste with sea salt and freshly ground black pepper. Serve with chutney, yoghurt and warm naan bread.

Chicken tagine with dates, lemon and pistachios

8 chicken thighs on the bone
  (about 1.5 kg/3 lb 5 oz), trimmed
  of excess fat, skin left on
2 onions, roughly chopped
3 garlic cloves
1 teaspoon sweet paprika
1 teaspoon ground ginger
2 teaspoons ground coriander
2 teaspoons ground cumin
1 long red chilli, chopped
½ teaspoon sea salt
80 ml (2½ fl oz/⅓ cup) olive oil
1 large handful coriander (cilantro)
  leaves, roughly chopped
1 large handful flat-leaf (Italian) parsley,
  roughly chopped
60 ml (2 fl oz/¼ cup) lemon juice
500 ml (17 fl oz/2 cups) chicken stock
1 carrot, cut into 8 cm (3¼ inch)
  matchsticks
150 g (5½ oz) green beans, trimmed
  and cut in half
150 g (5½ oz/1 cup) pitted dried dates,
  halved
185 g (6½ oz/1 cup) instant couscous
10 g (¼ oz) unsalted butter
35 g (1¼ oz/¼ cup) pistachio nuts
1 tablespoon finely chopped preserved
  lemon rind (optional)

Place the chicken thighs in a large bowl. Put the onion, garlic, spices, chilli, salt, half the olive oil, half the herbs and half the lemon juice in a food processor and blend until a paste forms. Pour the mixture over the chicken and toss to coat well. Cover and marinate in the refrigerator for at least 2 hours, or overnight.

Drain the chicken well, reserving the marinade. Heat the remaining oil in a large flameproof casserole dish over medium–high heat. Add half the chicken and cook for 2 minutes on each side to seal. Remove to a plate, then brown the remaining chicken.

Return all the chicken to the dish and add the reserved marinade, stock and carrot. Bring to the boil, reduce the heat to low, then cover and simmer for 20–25 minutes. Add the beans and dates and cook for 10 minutes, or until the chicken is tender and the vegetables are cooked through. Stir in the remaining lemon juice. Adjust the seasoning with sea salt if necessary.

Put the couscous in a large heatproof bowl and pour 375 ml (13 fl oz/1½ cups) boiling water over. Cover and leave to stand for 3 minutes, or until all the water has been absorbed. Stir in the butter, remaining herbs, pistachios and preserved lemon, if using. Fluff up the grains with a fork.

Divide the couscous among warm shallow bowls, top with the chicken mixture and serve.

Preparation time: 45 minutes
plus 2 hours (or overnight) marinating

Cooking time: 45 minutes

Serves: 4

Preparation time: 20 minutes
plus 20 minutes resting

Cooking time: 3 hours

Serves: 4

Veal and eggplant ragu with pappardelle

2 tablespoons olive oil

800 g (1 lb 12 oz) boned veal brisket, in one piece

1 onion, finely chopped

2 garlic cloves, crushed

a large pinch of chilli flakes

1 eggplant (aubergine), about 400 g (14 oz), cut into 3 cm (1¼ inch) lengths

1 tablespoon tomato paste (concentrated purée)

250 ml (9 fl oz/1 cup) white wine

1.25 litres (44 fl oz/5 cups) chicken stock, approximately

2 rosemary sprigs

1 teaspoon black peppercorns

500 g (1 lb 2 oz) fresh pappardelle

85 g (3 oz/½ cup) pitted kalamata olives

1 small handful flat-leaf (Italian) parsley, roughly chopped

50 g (1¾ oz/½ cup) shaved parmesan cheese

Heat half the olive oil in a large flameproof casserole dish over high heat. Add the veal brisket and cook for 3–4 minutes on each side, or until browned all over. Remove to a plate and set aside.

Heat the remaining oil in the casserole dish over medium heat. Add the onion, garlic and chilli flakes and sauté for 5–6 minutes, or until the onion has softened. Add the eggplant and cook for 3 minutes, or until well coated. Stir in the tomato paste and wine, scraping the bottom of the dish with a wooden spoon to loosen any cooked-on bits. Add 750 ml (26 fl oz/3 cups) of the stock, the rosemary sprigs and peppercorns and bring to the boil. Return the veal to the casserole. Cover, reduce the heat to very low and simmer for 2–2½ hours, or until the veal is very tender.

Remove the casserole dish from the heat. Transfer the veal to a plate and leave to rest for 20 minutes. Using two forks, shred the meat into 2 cm (¾ inch) chunks.

Meanwhile, add another 375 ml (13 fl oz/1½ cups) stock to the casserole dish and season the liquid to taste with sea salt and freshly ground black pepper. Place over medium–low heat and bring to a simmer. Using your hands, separate the pasta strands, then add to the liquid in the casserole. Cook for 8 minutes, or until the pasta is al dente, stirring constantly to stop the pasta sticking to the bottom of the dish; you may need to add a little more stock.

Add the shredded veal, olives and parsley and gently stir to combine. Divide among warm bowls and serve scattered with the parmesan.

Chicken and rice with lemongrass and ginger

Lap cheong are small Chinese sausages, mostly made of pork. They are air dried and therefore somewhat hard, with a distinctive, sweet flavour; they are sold in Asian supermarkets in vacuum packs. There is no real substitute for their flavour and unique texture, which softens considerably on steaming or gentle simmering. Generally they are not used whole, but are sliced or cut into small pieces. If you aren't able to obtain lap cheong, simply leave it out — the dish will still be delicious.

6 dried shiitake mushrooms
500 g (1 lb 2 oz) chicken thigh fillets, trimmed and cut into slices 1 cm (½ inch) thick
1 lemongrass stem, white part only, finely chopped
1.5 cm (⅝ inch) knob of fresh ginger, peeled and cut into thin matchsticks
1 garlic clove, chopped
60 ml (2 fl oz/¼ cup) oyster sauce
2 tablespoons soy sauce, plus extra, to serve (optional)
1 tablespoon cornflour (cornstarch)
1½ teaspoons sesame oil
2 Chinese pork sausages (lap cheong), about 60 g (2¼ oz), thinly sliced
300 g (10½ oz/1½ cups) long-grain white rice
2 spring onions (scallions), sliced

Put the mushrooms in a heatproof bowl and pour in enough boiling water to just cover. Leave to soak for 20 minutes, or until the mushrooms have softened. Drain well, discard the stems, then thinly slice the mushrooms.

Place the mushrooms in a bowl with the chicken, lemongrass, ginger, garlic, oyster sauce, soy sauce, cornflour, sesame oil and Chinese sausage. Mix well with clean hands until all the ingredients are well coated.

Wash the rice in several changes of cold water until the water runs almost clear. Place in a flameproof casserole dish with 750 ml (26 fl oz/3 cups) water. Cover, bring to the boil, then reduce the heat to a simmer. Once the rice begins to simmer, spread the chicken and sausage mixture on top of the rice. Cover and cook for 15–17 minutes, or until the liquid has been absorbed.

Remove the rice from the heat and leave to stand, covered, for 10 minutes. Mix together well, sprinkle with the spring onion and serve with extra soy sauce, if desired.

Preparation time: 15 minutes
plus 20 minutes soaking

Cooking time: 20 minutes

Serves: 4

Preparation time: 10 minutes   **Cooking time:** 50 minutes   **Serves:** 4–6

Japanese beef and potato stew (Niku jaga)

1 tablespoon vegetable oil
1 kg (2 lb 4 oz) beef rump, cut into
  3 cm (1¼ inch) chunks
1 onion, thinly sliced
2 carrots, cut into 1 cm (½ inch) rounds
2 red potatoes, peeled and cut into
  3 cm (1¼ inch) chunks
½ teaspoon dashi powder, mixed with
  250 ml (9 fl oz/1 cup) water
125 ml (4 fl oz/½ cup) mirin
2 tablespoons caster (superfine) sugar
60 ml (2 fl oz/¼ cup) Japanese soy sauce
200 g (7 oz) fresh udon noodles
2 spring onions (scallions), shredded on
  the diagonal

Heat the oil in a large heavy-based casserole dish over medium–high heat. Add the beef in batches and cook, turning often, until browned all over.

Add the onion, carrot, potato, dashi stock, mirin, sugar and 250 ml (9 fl oz/1 cup) water. Bring to the boil, reduce the heat to medium–low and simmer for 35 minutes, or until the beef and potatoes are tender.

Add the soy sauce and noodles, then cover and simmer for 3 minutes, or until the noodles are heated through.

Divide among warm bowls and serve sprinkled with the spring onion.

Dashi is an essential ingredient in Japanese cooking. It is a broth made by simmering kombu (a type of dried kelp) and shavings of dried, fermented tuna in water. It cannot be substituted with any other ingredient, but luckily instant dashi granules, which you dissolve in water, are widely sold in packets in the Asian section of larger supermarkets.

Spicy fish couscous

2 tablespoons olive oil
1 onion, chopped
2 garlic cloves, crushed
2 teaspoons Moroccan spice mix
    (available from supermarkets)
½ teaspoon chilli flakes
2 carrots, cut into 2 cm (¾ inch) chunks
1 red capsicum (pepper), cut into 2 cm
    (¾ inch) pieces
2 zucchini (courgettes), cut into 2 cm
    (¾ inch) chunks
750 ml (26 fl oz/ 3 cups) vegetable stock
750 g (1 lb 10 oz) boneless thick white
    fish fillets, cut into 2 cm (¾ inch)
    cubes
425 g (15 oz/ 2¼ cups) instant couscous
45 g (1½ oz/⅓ cup) pistachios, chopped
45 g (1½ oz/¼ cup) pitted green olives
1 small handful flat-leaf (Italian) parsley
2 teaspoons chopped preserved lemon
    rind (optional)
lemon wedges, to serve
harissa, to serve

Heat the olive oil in a large heavy-based saucepan. Add the onion, garlic, spice mix, chilli, carrot, capsicum and zucchini and sauté over low heat for 5 minutes, or until the vegetables are soft but not brown. Pour in the stock and bring to the boil, then reduce the heat, cover and simmer for 8 minutes, or until the vegetables are tender.

Add the fish and bring the mixture back to a simmer. Season with sea salt, then gently stir in the couscous using a wooden spoon, taking care not to break up the fish. Immediately remove the pan from the heat, then cover and leave to stand for 5 minutes.

Using a large fork, gently toss the couscous mixture to combine.

Divide among wide shallow bowls and sprinkle with the pistachios, olives, parsley and preserved lemon, if using. Serve with lemon wedges and some harissa.

Preparation time: 15 minutes   Cooking time: 20 minutes   Serves: 4–6

Iranian beef noodle soup

60 ml (2 fl oz/¼ cup) vegetable oil
2 large onions, thinly sliced
400 g (14 oz) gravy beef, trimmed of
   fat and sinew, cut into 1 cm (½ inch)
   chunks
400 g (14 oz) tin chickpeas, rinsed and
   drained
400 g (14 oz) tin white beans (such as
   cannellini), rinsed and drained
100 g (3½ oz/½ cup) yellow split peas
½ teaspoon ground turmeric
70 g (2½ oz/⅓ cup) dried apricots,
   roughly chopped
2 teaspoons finely grated orange rind
500 ml (17 fl oz/2 cups) beef stock
150 g (5½ oz) thin fresh egg noodles
   or linguine
1 large handful flat-leaf (Italian) parsley,
   finely chopped
1 large handful coriander (cilantro),
   finely chopped
1 large handful dill, finely chopped
250 g (9 oz/1 cup) Greek-style yoghurt
2 teaspoons mint, torn
warmed Turkish bread, to serve

Heat 2 tablespoons of the oil in a large, heavy-based saucepan over medium heat. Add the onion and sauté for 8–10 minutes, or until golden. Remove to a small bowl.

Heat half the remaining oil in the pan. Working in batches, add the beef to the pan and brown each batch for 3 minutes, or until sealed all over, adding the remaining oil to the pan as needed.

Return all the meat to the pan and add half the onion and all the chickpeas, beans, split peas, turmeric, apricots and orange rind. Stir well and season with freshly ground black pepper. Pour in the stock and 1 litre (35 fl oz/4 cups) water and bring to the boil. Reduce the heat to medium–low and simmer for 30–40 minutes, or until the beef and split peas are tender.

Increase the heat to a simmer. Season the soup with sea salt and add a little extra water if necessary. Stir in the noodles and cook for 8 minutes, or until al dente. Stir in the parsley, coriander and dill.

Divide the soup among warm deep bowls. Spoon some yoghurt on top of each bowl and scatter with the remaining sautéed onion. Scatter the mint over the top and serve immediately, with warm Turkish bread to pass around.

Saffron chicken with fennel and green olive tapénade

Although saffron is a costly spice, a little goes a very long way and nothing else compares to its warm, mellow flavour or the lovely golden colour it imparts. You can buy saffron in powdered form or as threads; the threads (which are actually the dried stamens of a type of crocus flower) give the best flavour.

2½ tablespoons olive oil
1 large (1.9 kg/4 lb 3 oz) whole chicken, cut into 8 pieces
1 leek, white part only, trimmed and cut into 2 cm (¾ inch) rounds
2 onions, cut into wedges
1 fennel bulb, trimmed and cut into wedges
2 carrots, cut into 1 cm (½ inch) rounds
2 celery stalks, cut into 2 cm (¾ inch) chunks
a large pinch of saffron threads
2 garlic cloves, thinly sliced
1.5 litres (52 fl oz/6 cups) chicken stock
grated rind of 1 lemon
2½ tablespoons lemon juice
8 baby new potatoes (about 500 g/ 1 lb 2 oz), halved
1 handful flat-leaf (Italian) parsley, chopped
crusty bread, to serve

Green olive tapénade
75 g (2½ oz/½ cup) pimento-stuffed green olives
1 garlic clove
1 tablespoon capers in brine, rinsed and drained
2 anchovy fillets
1 small handful flat-leaf (Italian) parsley
125 ml (4 fl oz/½ cup) olive oil

Heat the olive oil in a large flameproof casserole dish. Add the chicken pieces, in batches if necessary, and cook, turning often, for 5–6 minutes, or until browned all over.

Return all the chicken pieces to the casserole dish. Add the leek, onion, fennel, carrot, celery, saffron, garlic, stock, lemon rind, lemon juice and potatoes. Bring to the boil, skimming off any froth that rises to the surface, then reduce the heat to low and gently simmer for 50 minutes, or until the chicken is just cooked through, skimming occasionally.

Meanwhile, make the tapénade. Put the olives, garlic, capers, anchovies and parsley in a food processor. Pulse to roughly chop the ingredients, then season with freshly ground black pepper. Add the olive oil and blend until combined.

Stir the parsley through the stew, then divide the chicken, vegetables and cooking liquid among warm deep bowls. Spoon the tapénade over and serve with crusty bread.

✳ **Preparation time:** 25 minutes ✳ **Cooking time:** 1 hour ✳ **Serves:** 4

Slow-braised spiced beef with prunes and silverbeet

80 ml (2½ fl oz/⅓ cup) olive oil

1.25 kg (2 lb 12 oz) chuck or other braising beef steak, trimmed and cut into 4 cm (1½ inch) chunks

2 onions, chopped

2 carrots, cut into 2 cm (¾ inch) chunks

2 garlic cloves, crushed

1 teaspoon ground mixed spice (allspice)

1 teaspoon ground cinnamon

2 teaspoons ground turmeric

1 teaspoon ground cumin

100 g (3½ oz/½ cup) pitted prunes, chopped

1 tomato, chopped

1 litre (35 fl oz/4 cups) chicken stock, approximately

3 desiree potatoes (about 500 g/ 1 lb 2 oz), peeled and cut into 4 cm (1½ inch) chunks

350 g (12 oz/½ small bunch) silverbeet (Swiss chard), stems removed, leaves washed, dried and chopped

coriander (cilantro) leaves, to serve

Greek-style yoghurt, to serve

Heat 2 tablespoons of the olive oil in a flameproof casserole dish or large heavy-based saucepan over medium heat. Add the beef in batches, and cook, turning often, for 3–4 minutes each time, or until browned all over. Remove each batch to a plate and set aside.

Heat the remaining oil in the pan and sauté the onion, carrot and garlic for 2 minutes, or until the onion starts to soften. Stir in the spices and cook for 1 minute, or until aromatic, stirring to coat the onion. Add the prunes, tomato, beef and enough stock to cover the mixture. Bring to a simmer, then cover and cook over low heat for 1½ hours, or until the beef is tender.

Add the potatoes and simmer for a further 30–40 minutes, or until the potatoes are tender. Stir the silverbeet through, then remove from the heat, cover and rest for 5 minutes before serving.

Spoon the mixture into warmed wide shallow bowls. Scatter with coriander leaves, drizzle with yoghurt and serve.

Seafood and sausage gumbo

2 tablespoons vegetable oil

2 smoked pork sausages (such as kransky sausages), casings removed, meat chopped

2 garlic cloves, crushed

1 carrot, chopped

1 celery stalk, thinly sliced

1 red capsicum (pepper), cut into 1 cm (½ inch) chunks

1 teaspoon sweet smoked paprika

½ teaspoon cayenne pepper

60 g (2¼ oz) butter

60 g (2¼ oz/heaped ⅓ cup) plain (all-purpose) flour

625 ml (21½ fl oz/2½ cups) fish stock

400 g (14 oz) tin chopped tomatoes

200 g (7 oz) raw king prawns (shrimp), peeled, deveined and cut into thirds

400 g (14 oz) firm white fish fillets (such as ling, basa or monk fish)

10 shucked oysters

150 g (5½ oz) fresh or tinned crabmeat, drained

finely grated rind of 1 lemon

chopped parsley, to serve

crusty bread, to serve

Heat the oil in a large heavy-based saucepan over medium heat. Add the sausage meat and sauté for 3–4 minutes, or until lightly browned. Add the garlic, carrot, celery and capsicum and sauté for 4–5 minutes, or until the vegetables have softened. Add the paprika and cayenne pepper and cook for 30 seconds, or until fragrant. Remove the mixture from the pan and set aside.

Melt the butter in the pan, then add the flour and stir until smooth. Cook, stirring often, for 4–5 minutes, or until the mixture is browned and smells toasted; take care not to let it burn. Pour in the stock and cook for 20 minutes, stirring frequently to prevent lumps forming, until the mixture thickens slightly.

Stir in 500 ml (17 fl oz/2 cups) water, the tomatoes and the sausage and vegetable mixture. Increase the heat to high and bring the mixture to the boil, then reduce the heat to low and simmer for 1 hour, stirring occasionally.

Stir in the prawns and fish and cook for 5 minutes, then stir in the oysters, crab and lemon rind and cook for another minute, or until the seafood is heated through. Ladle into warm deep bowls, sprinkle with parsley and serve with crusty bread.

Preparation time: 30 minutes   **Cooking time:** 1 hour 40 minutes   **Serves:** 4

Preparation time: 20 minutes   **Cooking time:** 1 hour 50 minutes   **Serves:** 4–6

Cameroon pork curry

40 g (1½ oz) butter
1 onion, chopped
3 garlic cloves, crushed
2 tablespoons Indian-style curry powder
1 teaspoon chilli flakes
1.25 kg (2 lb 12 oz) pork shoulder or
  leg, trimmed and cut into 2 cm
  (¾ inch) chunks
400 ml (14 fl oz) tin coconut cream
1 sweet potato (200 g/7 oz), peeled
  and cut into 2 cm (¾ inch) chunks
½ small ripe sweet pineapple,
  trimmed, cored and cut into 2 cm
  (¾ inch) chunks
1 green capsicum (pepper), cut into
  1 cm (½ inch) dice
30 g (1 oz/½ cup) shredded coconut
1 banana, peeled and chopped
1 mango, peeled and diced
40 g (1½ oz/¼ cup) roasted peanuts,
  chopped
1 small handful coriander (cilantro) leaves
naan bread, to serve

Melt the butter in a large heavy-based saucepan or flameproof casserole dish over medium heat. Add the onion and sauté for 5 minutes, or until softened. Add the garlic, curry powder and chilli flakes and cook, stirring often, for 3 minutes, or until fragrant.

Add the pork and toss well to coat in the spices. Cover and cook over very low heat for 10 minutes, stirring often. Add the coconut cream, then cover and slowly simmer for 1 hour. Stir in the sweet potato, pineapple and capsicum, then cover and simmer over low heat for 30 minutes, or until the pork is tender and the vegetables are cooked through.

Put the shredded coconut in a small bowl and roll the banana in the coconut to coat. Put the mango and peanuts in separate small bowls to serve as garnishes for the curry.

Sprinkle the curry with the coriander and serve with the banana, mango, peanuts and naan bread.

If fresh mangoes are not in season, use a drained 400 g (14 oz) tin of mangoes instead.

Penne with pesto, bocconcini and cherry tomatoes

For extra flavour, add some semi-dried (sun-blushed) tomatoes as well. For anchovy lovers, add 4 anchovies to the olive oil before frying the tomatoes — and for chilli lovers add some chilli flakes to taste. For a meat version, add 150 g (5½ oz) diced salami or ham.

500 g (1 lb 2 oz) penne pasta
1 tablespoon extra virgin olive oil
250 g (9 oz) cherry tomatoes, halved
190 g (7 oz) jar pesto
2 large handfuls baby English
  spinach leaves
1 small handful basil, roughly chopped
60 ml (2 fl oz/¼ cup) cream
25 g (1 oz/¼ cup) grated parmesan
  cheese, plus extra, to serve
1 garlic clove, crushed
2 tablespoons pine nuts
1 teaspoon finely grated lemon rind
180 g (6 oz) bocconcini (fresh baby
  mozzarella cheese), torn

Bring a large saucepan of salted water to the boil. Add the pasta and cook according to the packet instructions, until al dente. Drain well and set aside.

Place the saucepan back over medium heat. Add the olive oil and tomatoes and cook for 2–3 minutes, or until the tomatoes have softened slightly. Add the pesto, drained pasta, spinach leaves, basil, cream and parmesan. Cook for 3–5 minutes, or until heated through, stirring to combine well.

Remove from the heat, then add the garlic, pine nuts, lemon rind and bocconcini, tossing to combine well.

Season to taste with sea salt and freshly ground black pepper and divide among warm bowls. Sprinkle with extra parmesan and serve.

Preparation time: 10 minutes   Cooking time: 20 minutes   Serves: 4–6

Preparation time: 20 minutes
plus 30 minutes chilling

Cooking time: 40 minutes

Serves: 6

Mexican meatball soup

2 tablespoons olive oil
1 onion, finely chopped
1 garlic clove, chopped
1 teaspoon ground cumin
250 ml (9 fl oz/1 cup) ready-made
   Mexican salsa
400 g (14 oz) tin chopped tomatoes
1 litre (35 fl oz/4 cups) beef stock
400 g (14 oz) tin red kidney beans,
   rinsed and drained
1 small handful coriander (cilantro)
   leaves, chopped
60 g (2¼ oz/½ cup) grated cheddar
   cheese
sour cream, to serve
corn chips, to serve (optional)

Meatballs
500 g (1 lb 2 oz) minced (ground) beef
60 g (2¼ oz/½ cup) grated cheddar
   cheese
40 g (1½ oz/½ cup) fresh breadcrumbs
2 egg yolks
1 garlic clove, chopped
1 small handful coriander (cilantro)
   leaves, chopped
2 tablespoons lime juice
½ teaspoon ground chilli, or to taste
1 teaspoon dried oregano
1 teaspoon ground cumin

For the meatballs, combine all the ingredients in a bowl and season well with sea salt and freshly ground black pepper. Using wet hands, roll heaped teaspoons of the mixture into balls. Place on a tray, cover with plastic wrap and refrigerate for 30 minutes, or until required.

Heat 1½ tablespoons of the olive oil in a large non-stick saucepan over medium–high heat. Cook the meatballs in batches, turning regularly, for 2–3 minutes, or until golden. Set aside.

Heat the remaining oil in the pan. Add the onion and sauté for 4–5 minutes, or until softened. Add the garlic and cumin and cook for another minute. Stir in the salsa, tomatoes, stock and kidney beans. Bring to the boil, then reduce the heat to medium and simmer for 15 minutes. Add the meatballs and coriander and simmer for 5 minutes, or until the meatballs are heated through.

Divide the soup and meatballs among warm bowls. Scatter with the cheese, add a dollop of sour cream and serve with corn chips, if desired.

This soup can be prepared ahead of time if you don't add the meatballs. Instead, reheat the soup and add the meatballs and coriander 5 minutes before serving.

Seafood fideus

60 ml (2 fl oz/¼ cup) olive oil
250 g (9 oz) angel hair pasta,
  roughly broken
1 onion, quartered
500 g (1 lb 2 oz) ripe tomatoes,
  roughly chopped
2 garlic cloves, peeled
1½ teaspoons ground sweet paprika
a pinch of chilli flakes
625 ml (21½ fl oz/2½ cups) chicken or
  vegetable stock
a large pinch of saffron threads (optional)
12 mussels, bearded and scrubbed
12 raw king prawns (shrimp), peeled
  and deveined, tails left intact
300 g (10½ oz) cleaned small squid
  tubes, cut into rings
1 small handful coriander (cilantro) leaves

Heat half the olive oil in a large (26 cm/
10½ inch), deep heavy-based frying pan. Add
the pasta pieces and stir for 2–3 minutes, or
until light brown all over. Remove from the pan
and set aside.

Put the onion, tomatoes, garlic, paprika
and chilli flakes in a food processor and pulse
until finely chopped but not puréed. Heat the
remaining oil in the frying pan and add the
tomato mixture. Cook over medium heat for
10–12 minutes, or until the mixture has
thickened a little, stirring often.

Stir in the stock, saffron if using, and pasta,
pushing the pasta down so it is covered with
liquid. Bring the mixture to the boil, then reduce
the heat to medium–low and cook for 5 minutes.

Add all the seafood, pushing the pieces into
the mixture to cover them well. Cook for a further
5–8 minutes, or until the seafood is cooked and
the mussels have opened — discard any mussels
that don't open. By now the liquid should be
absorbed and the pasta cooked.

Season to taste with sea salt and freshly
ground black pepper, sprinkle with the coriander,
divide among warm bowls and serve at once.

☀ Preparation time: 20 minutes   **☀ Cooking time:** 30 minutes   **☀ Serves:** 4

Spanish pork casserole

2 tablespoons vegetable oil

750 g (1 lb 10 oz) pork neck, trimmed and cut into 3–4 cm (1¼–1½ inch) chunks

1 large red onion, cut into 2 cm (¾ inch) wedges

1 mild chorizo sausage (150 g/5½ oz), cut into 1 cm (½ inch) slices

2 garlic cloves, crushed

5 thyme sprigs, plus extra, to garnish

1 tablespoon smoked paprika

125 ml (4 fl oz/½ cup) dry sherry

250 g (9 oz/1 cup) bottled marinated roasted red capsicum (pepper) strips, drained

400 g (14 oz) tin chopped tomatoes

500 ml (17 fl oz/2 cups) chicken stock

85 g (3 oz/½ cup) pitted green olives

400 g (14 oz) tin chickpeas, rinsed and drained

115 g (4 oz/½ cup) medium-grain brown rice

150 g (5½ oz) green beans, trimmed and sliced into thirds

Heat the oil in a large flameproof casserole dish over medium–high heat. Season the pork with sea salt and freshly ground black pepper, then add to the casserole dish in batches and cook for 2–3 minutes on each side, or until golden brown. Remove to a plate and set aside.

Reduce the heat to medium. Add the onion and chorizo to the casserole dish and sauté for 4–5 minutes, or until golden. Add the garlic, thyme and paprika and sauté for a further minute. Pour in the sherry, bring to the boil and cook until the liquid has reduced by half.

Add the pork (and any juices) to the casserole with the capsicum, tomatoes, stock, olives, chickpeas and rice. Bring the mixture to a simmer, then reduce the heat to very low. Cover and simmer for 1 hour.

Add the beans and stir gently to combine. Cover and simmer for another 25 minutes, or until the pork is tender and the beans are cooked through. Garnish with thyme sprigs and serve.

Tinned white beans can be used instead of chickpeas — just add them to the pot when adding the green beans. Frozen green peas or broad (fava) beans can be used instead of the green beans; simply add them 5 minutes before the end of cooking. This casserole will freeze well in a sealed container for up to 1 month.

Chicken, sausage and corn soup

You can add a small handful of very finely shredded iceberg lettuce to each bowl before ladling in the hot soup.

1.25 kg (2 lb 12 oz) chicken thighs on the bone, trimmed of excess fat, skin left on
200 g (7 oz/1 cup) medium-grain white rice, washed
1 tablespoon finely shredded fresh ginger
3 teaspoons Chinese rice wine
2 teaspoons Chinese rice vinegar
3 teaspoons soy sauce
1½ teaspoons caster (superfine) sugar
1 teaspoon sesame oil
3 Chinese pork sausages (lap cheong), about 100 g (3½ oz), available from Asian food stores (see page 20)
400 g (14 oz) tin corn kernels, drained
ground white pepper, to taste
1 small handful chopped coriander (cilantro)
1 spring onion (scallion), thinly sliced
50 g (1¾ oz/⅓ cup) chopped roasted unsalted peanuts, to serve

Put the chicken thighs in a large heavy-based saucepan. Pour in 1.5 litres (52 fl oz/6 cups) water, adding a little extra water to cover the chicken if necessary. Bring the water to a simmer, skimming off any froth that rises to the surface. Reduce the heat to low and cook, uncovered, for 1½ hours, or until the chicken is very tender, skimming often. Remove the chicken to a bowl and set aside to cool.

Skim as much fat as possible from the chicken broth. Stir in the rice, ginger and 1.5 litres (52 fl oz/6 cups) water and bring to a simmer. Reduce the heat to low, then partially cover and simmer for 2 hours, or until the rice is very soft and breaking up and the mixture is the consistency of thin porridge — you may need to add more water now and then during cooking.

Meanwhile, when the chicken is cool enough to handle, remove and discard the skin and bones. Using your fingers, finely shred the meat, then combine in a bowl with the rice wine, rice vinegar, soy sauce, sugar and sesame oil. Toss to combine well, then cover and set aside.

When the rice is very soft, very thinly slice the sausages and add to the soup. Cook for 2–3 minutes. Add the chicken mixture and corn, stir to combine well, then season to taste with sea salt and ground white pepper. Bring the mixture just to a simmer and cook over low heat for 2–3 minutes, or until the sausage is cooked and the chicken is heated through.

Divide the soup among large warm bowls. Sprinkle with the coriander, spring onion and peanuts and serve immediately.

✳ **Preparation time:** 35 minutes   ✳ **Cooking time:** 3 hours 45 minutes   ✳ **Serves:** 6

45 ONE-POT WONDERS

Preparation time: 25 minutes   **Cooking time:** 1 hour 45 minutes   **Serves:** 4–6

Beef braciola

6 topside steaks, each 1 cm (½ inch)
   thick (about 1 kg/2 lb 4 oz in total),
   trimmed
2 tablespoons olive oil
1 onion, chopped
1 carrot, cut into 1 cm (½ inch) rounds
1 bay leaf
185 ml (6 fl oz/¾ cup) red wine
250 ml (9 fl oz/1 cup) beef stock
2 potatoes, peeled and cut into 3 cm
   (1¼ inch) chunks

Stuffing
2 tablespoons chopped parsley
2 tablespoons shredded basil
2 garlic cloves, crushed
120 g (4¼ oz/1½ cups) fresh
   breadcrumbs
1 egg, lightly beaten
50 g (1¾ oz/½ cup) grated parmesan
   cheese
4 anchovy fillets, finely chopped
35 g (1¼ oz/¼ cup) chopped raisins

For the stuffing, combine all the ingredients in a bowl and season with sea salt and freshly ground black pepper. Mix together well, then divide the mixture evenly among the six steaks, placing the stuffing along a wide end of each steak. Roll the steaks up tightly, then secure with toothpicks so they hold a neat shape.

Heat the olive oil in a large heavy-based frying pan over medium–high heat. Cook the beef rolls for 3–5 minutes, turning often, until browned all over. Remove to a plate and cover with foil.

Reheat the frying pan and sauté the onion, carrot and bay leaf for 5 minutes, or until the onion is lightly browned. Pour in the wine and stock and bring to the boil, then reduce the heat to a low simmer.

Return the beef rolls to the pan with any juices. Season well, then cover and cook over low heat for 1 hour. Add the potato and cook for another 30 minutes, or until the beef is tender and the sauce has reduced.

To serve, remove the beef rolls and cut them on the diagonal. Divide the vegetable mixture among warm shallow bowls, top with the beef rolls and spoon the sauce over.

In the stuffing, instead of the anchovies you can use some chopped semi-dried (sun-blushed) tomatoes or toasted pine nuts.

Tuscan-style ribollita

Ribollita is a traditional Italian 'meal-in-a-bowl' soup and is an excellent way to use up left-over bread. Make sure though that you use a good, slightly stale, rustic-style bread with plenty of body and flavour, such as ciabatta — sliced supermarket bread will not give the right taste or texture here. This soup freezes well without the bread; add the bread once the frozen soup has been thawed and reheated.

60 ml (2 fl oz/¼ cup) extra virgin olive oil
1 onion, cut into 1 cm (½ inch) chunks
1 carrot, cut into 1 cm (½ inch) chunks
40 g (1½ oz) pancetta, chopped
2 garlic cloves, crushed
¼ small green cabbage (about 250 g/
  9 oz), core and tough outer leaves
  discarded, leaves roughly chopped
1 tablespoon tomato paste (concentrated
  purée)
400 g (14 oz) tin chopped tomatoes
400 g (14 oz/½ bunch) silverbeet
  (Swiss chard), stems removed, leaves
  washed, dried and thinly sliced
400 g (14 oz) tin cannellini beans,
  rinsed and drained
750 ml (26 fl oz/3 cups) chicken stock
1 bay leaf
3 cm (1¼ inch) piece of parmesan
  cheese rind
200 g (7 oz) piece of day-old rustic-style
  bread, torn into 1 cm (½ inch) chunks
  (about 2 cups)
65 g (2½ oz/⅔ cup) shaved parmesan
  cheese

Heat the olive oil in a large heavy-based saucepan over medium heat. Add the onion, carrot, pancetta, garlic and cabbage and sauté for 7 minutes, or until the vegetables are lightly golden.

Stir in the tomato paste, tomatoes and silverbeet, then the beans, stock, bay leaf and parmesan rind. Bring the soup just to a simmer, then cook over low heat for 30 minutes, or until the vegetables are very tender.

Stir in the bread chunks, then cover and leave for 2–3 minutes, or until the bread is soft.

Divide the soup among warm deep bowls. Scatter the shaved parmesan over the soup and serve immediately.

Preparation time: 15 minutes   **Cooking time:** 1 hour 10 minutes   **Serves:** 4–6

Chicken mole

1 tablespoon olive oil
8 chicken thigh fillets,
  trimmed and cut in half widthways
1 tablespoon unsweetened cocoa powder
400 g (14 oz) tin chopped tomatoes
500 ml (17 fl oz/2 cups) chicken stock
1 handful coriander (cilantro) leaves,
  roughly chopped, plus extra, to serve
warmed soft tortillas, to serve
chopped avocado, to serve
sour cream, to serve

Spice paste
1 tablespoon olive oil
1 onion, chopped
2 garlic cloves, crushed
½ teaspoon chilli flakes
1 teaspoon ground cumin
1 teaspoon ground cinnamon
1 teaspoon ground coriander
1 green capsicum (pepper), chopped
60 g (2¼ oz/¼ cup) almond butter

For the spice paste, put all the ingredients in a food processor and blend to a smooth paste. Set aside.

Heat the olive oil in a large heavy-based saucepan dish over medium heat. Add the chicken in batches and cook for 2 minutes on each side, or until golden, removing each batch to a plate.

Add the spice paste to the pan and sauté over medium–low heat for 4–5 minutes, or until fragrant and aromatic. Stir in the cocoa powder, tomatoes and stock. Return all the chicken to the pan and bring the mixture to a simmer. Reduce the heat to low and simmer for 50 minutes, or until the sauce is thick and the chicken is cooked through.

Stir in the coriander and season to taste with sea salt and freshly ground black pepper. Sprinkle with some extra coriander and serve with some warm tortillas, with the avocado and sour cream passed separately.

Almond butter is a paste made from almonds, similar to peanut butter. You'll find it in health food stores.

Soba noodle soup with salmon

Instead of salmon you can use thinly sliced chicken, beef rib eye or scotch fillet — or for a vegetarian option, use sliced tofu. Soba noodles (Japanese buckwheat noodles), dashi powder (Japanese soup stock), mirin (sweet Japanese rice wine) and miso paste are available from Asian food stores and many major supermarkets.

270 g (9½ oz) packet dried soba noodles
2½ teaspoons dashi powder
60 ml (2 fl oz/¼ cup) mirin
60 ml (2 fl oz/¼ cup) soy sauce
6 fresh shiitake mushrooms, trimmed and sliced
3 cm (1¼ inch) knob of fresh ginger, peeled and cut into thin matchsticks
2 tablespoons white miso paste
500 g (1 lb 2 oz) salmon fillets, skin and bones removed, flesh cut into 2 cm (¾ inch) cubes
1 large handful English spinach leaves, washed, dried and roughly torn
4 spring onions (scallions), thinly sliced on the diagonal

Bring a large saucepan of water to the boil over medium heat. Add the noodles and stir to separate. Return to the boil, then add 750 ml (26 fl oz/3 cups) cold water and bring back just to a simmer. Cook for 1–2 minutes, or until the noodles are just tender. Drain well, rinse under cold water and set aside.

Pour 2 litres (70 fl oz/8 cups) water into a large saucepan and add the dashi powder, mirin, soy sauce, mushrooms, ginger and miso paste. Place over medium heat and bring to the boil, then reduce the heat to low and simmer for 3 minutes, or until the miso has dissolved. Add the salmon and simmer for 2 minutes, then add the noodles and remove from the heat.

Divide the spinach leaves among four warm bowls and sprinkle with the spring onion. Ladle the soup broth, salmon and noodles over the spinach and serve.

Preparation time: 15 minutes   **Cooking time:** 15 minutes   **Serves:** 4

Preparation time: 25 minutes **Cooking time:** 20 minutes **Serves:** 4–6

Prawn and lime pilaff

300 g (10½ oz/1½ cups) jasmine rice
85 g (3 oz/1 bunch) coriander (cilantro)
1 tablespoon peanut or vegetable oil
4 spring onions (scallions), thinly sliced
1 tablespoon finely chopped fresh ginger
560 ml (19¼ fl oz/2¼ cups) chicken stock
2 tablespoons fish sauce
finely grated rind of 1 lime
1½ tablespoons lime juice
1 lemongrass stem, white part only,
   thinly sliced
150 g (5½ oz/about 1 bunch) snake
   (yard-long) beans, cut into 5 mm
   (¼ inch) lengths
300 g (10½ oz) small cleaned squid
   tubes, cut into strips measuring about
   1 x 5 cm (½ x 2 inches)
700 g (1 lb 9 oz) raw king prawns
   (shrimp), peeled and deveined, then
   cut in half lengthways
50 g (1¾ oz/⅓ cup) cashew nuts
4 kaffir lime leaves, finely shredded
lime wedges, to serve

Put the rice in a large heavy-based saucepan and shake, uncovered, over low heat for 4 minutes, or until the rice is lightly toasted and fragrant. Remove the rice to a plate and leave the pan to cool for a few minutes.

Rinse the coriander bunch well, then trim and discard the roots. Finely slice the coriander stalks; shred the leaves and reserve as a garnish.

Heat the oil in the saucepan over medium–low heat. Add the coriander stalks, spring onion and ginger and sauté for 2–3 minutes, or until softened. Add the rice, stock, fish sauce, lime rind, lime juice and lemongrass and bring to the boil. Cover, reduce the heat to low and simmer for 7 minutes.

Add the snake beans, squid and prawns, then cover and cook for another 3 minutes. Without removing the lid, remove the pan from the heat and leave to stand for 5 minutes — the rice and seafood should be tender and the liquid absorbed.

Divide the pilaff among warm bowls. Garnish with the cashews, lime leaves and reserved coriander leaves and serve with lime wedges.

To shred a kaffir lime leaf, fold the leaf in half down the centre vein and cut the vein away using a large sharp knife. Stack the trimmed leaves on top of each other, roll them up tightly and cut into fine strips. If fresh kaffir lime leaves are not available, use dried whole leaves (available from Asian food stores), but remove them from the pilaff before serving. Fresh kaffir lime leaves can be frozen for later use.

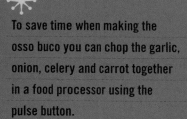

To save time when making the osso buco you can chop the garlic, onion, celery and carrot together in a food processor using the pulse button.

Osso buco with potatoes and orange olive gremolata

6 even-sized pieces of veal osso buco
  (about 1 kg/2 lb 4 oz), each about
  4 cm (1½ inches) thick
1 tablespoon plain (all-purpose) flour
1 tablespoon olive oil
20 g (¾ oz) butter
1 onion, finely chopped
2 garlic cloves, finely chopped
1 celery stalk, finely chopped
1 carrot, finely chopped
2 strips orange zest, each about 1 cm
  (½ inch) wide, all white pith removed
250 ml (9 fl oz/1 cup) white wine
6 small new potatoes (about 350 g/
  12 oz in total), halved
250 ml (9 fl oz/1 cup) chicken stock

Orange olive gremolata
2 tablespoons finely chopped parsley
2 teaspoons finely grated orange rind
1 garlic clove, finely chopped
60 g (2¼ oz/⅓ cup) pitted green olives,
  rinsed and very finely chopped

Pat the veal pieces dry with paper towels and dust with the flour, shaking off any excess. Heat the olive oil in a large heavy-based casserole dish that is deep enough to fit all the veal and potatoes in a single layer. Add the veal pieces and cook over medium heat, turning once, for 5 minutes, or until browned. Remove to a plate.

Melt the butter in the casserole dish over low heat. Add the onion, garlic, celery, carrot and orange zest and sauté for 5 minutes, or until the vegetables are soft but not browned. Stir in the wine and bring to a simmer, then cover the dish and reduce the heat to low. Allow to simmer for 10 minutes, then place the veal and potatoes over the mixture in a single layer. Pour in the stock, then cover and simmer for 40 minutes.

Carefully turn the potatoes and veal over and add a little stock or water if needed to keep them covered. Cover and simmer for a further 15–20 minutes, or until the meat and potatoes are tender.

Just before serving, put all the gremolata ingredients in a small bowl and stir to mix well.

Remove the veal pieces carefully to a large plate, cover with foil and keep warm. (If there is too much liquid in the dish, remove the potatoes and keep warm; boil the sauce until reduced slightly.) Remove and discard the orange zest. Stir half the gremolata through the sauce and scatter the rest over the top.

Divide the veal among warm plates, spoon the sauce and potatoes over and serve.

Preparation time: 25 minutes   **Cooking time:** 15 minutes   **Serves:** 4

Pork won ton soup

400 g (14 oz) minced (ground) pork

200 g (7 oz) raw prawns (shrimp),
   peeled, deveined and chopped

1½ teaspoons sesame oil

1 tablespoon soy sauce, plus extra,
   to serve (optional)

1 tablespoon oyster sauce

1 tablespoon cornflour (cornstarch)

2 spring onions (scallions), sliced

250 g (9 oz) packet won ton wrappers

2 litres (70 fl oz/8 cups) chicken stock

180 g (6 oz) fresh egg noodles

3 baby bok choy (pak choy), trimmed
   and roughly chopped

100 g (3½ oz) fresh shiitake or oyster
   mushrooms, sliced

hot chilli sauce, to serve (optional)

Put the pork, prawns, sesame oil, soy sauce, oyster sauce, cornflour and half the spring onion in a bowl. Using your hands, knead the mixture together until it feels slightly elastic. Place heaped teaspoons of the mixture on the won ton wrappers, lightly brush the edges with water, then fold up the corners of each wrapper to enclose the filling.

Bring the stock to the boil in a large saucepan. Add the won tons in two batches and cook for 5 minutes each time, or until they rise to the surface. Remove using a slotted spoon and divide among large warm deep bowls.

Bring the stock back to the boil, if necessary, then add the noodles and cook for 1–2 minutes. Add the bok choy and mushrooms and cook for a further 1–2 minutes, or until the bok choy begins to wilt.

Divide the hot broth, noodles and vegetables among the bowls. Sprinkle with the remaining spring onion and serve immediately, with chilli sauce and extra soy sauce, if desired.

The won tons can be made up to 2 hours in advance. Place them in a single layer on a tray lined with baking paper and cover with plastic wrap until you are ready to cook them. For best results, use homemade chicken stock in this recipe.

Madrid cocido

Traditionally, the broth from this dish is served as a separate course. The finished dish can be as soupy or as dry as you like. If you have too much stock remaining after cooking, reduce the liquid in a saucepan over high heat. For a quick tomato salad to accompany the cocido, cut 4 ripe roma (plum) tomatoes into chunks and gently toss in a bowl with 2 tablespoons extra virgin olive oil, 1 tablespoon sherry or white wine vinegar, and sea salt to taste.

1.4 kg (3 lb 2 oz) corn-fed chicken, cut in half through the breast and backbone
200 g (7 oz) piece of smoked streaky bacon
1 onion, studded with 4 cloves
500 ml (17 fl oz/2 cups) chicken stock
2 leeks, white part only, washed well and sliced 2 cm (¾ inch) thick
2 tomatoes, skinned and quartered
2 x 400 g (14 oz) tins chickpeas, rinsed and drained
150 g (5½ oz) green beans, trimmed and halved
2 chorizo sausages (about 200 g/7 oz in total), each sliced into thirds
500 g (1 lb 2 oz/1 bunch) English spinach, trimmed, washed and chopped
extra virgin olive oil, to drizzle (optional)

Put the chicken, bacon and onion in a large heavy-based saucepan. Pour in the stock and enough cold water to cover the meat. Bring to the boil, skimming off any froth that rises to the surface, then reduce the heat to low and simmer gently for 30 minutes.

Stir in the leek and tomatoes and simmer for 20 minutes. Add the chickpeas, beans and chorizo and simmer for another 10 minutes, or until the meat and vegetables are tender. Add the spinach and cook for 1–2 minutes, or until just wilted, then season to taste with sea salt and freshly ground black pepper.

Remove and discard the onion. Remove and reserve the chicken, chorizo and bacon. Cut the bacon into chunks and cut the chicken into serving pieces.

Divide the meats among warm wide serving bowls. Using a slotted spoon, lift the chickpeas and vegetables from the broth and pile them on top of the meats. Drizzle with olive oil, if desired. Strain the liquid into separate bowls and serve.

✳ **Preparation time:** 20 minutes ✳ **Cooking time:** 1 hour 10 minutes ✳ **Serves:** 6

Preparation time: 25 minutes
plus 10 minutes chilling

Cooking time: 30 minutes

Serves: 6

Avgolemono with chicken meatballs

250 ml (9 fl oz/1 cup) cream
4 egg yolks
2 celery stalks, finely diced
400 g (14 oz) red potatoes, peeled
   and cut into 2 cm (¾ inch) dice
1.5 litres (52 fl oz/6 cups) chicken stock
400 g (14 oz) tin white beans, rinsed
   and drained
1 teaspoon finely grated lemon rind
125 ml (4 fl oz/½ cup) lemon juice
1 small handful flat-leaf (Italian)
   parsley, chopped

Chicken meatballs

500 g (1 lb 2 oz) minced (ground)
   chicken
1 small handful flat-leaf (Italian)
   parsley, chopped
¼ teaspoon dried oregano
1 egg

For the chicken meatballs, put all the ingredients in a bowl and season with sea salt and freshly ground black pepper. Mix well, using your hands. Roll tablespoons of the mixture into small balls. Place on a tray, then cover and refrigerate for 10 minutes.

In a small bowl, whisk together the cream and egg yolks. Set aside.

Put the celery and potatoes in a large heavy-based saucepan. Pour in the stock. Bring to the boil and cook for 10–15 minutes, or until the potato is tender. Stir in the beans.

Bring the soup back to the boil and add the meatballs. Reduce the heat to low and simmer for 5 minutes, or until the meatballs are cooked through. Remove the soup from the heat, then carefully stir the egg mixture through.

Return the soup to low heat for 2 minutes, stirring constantly. The soup will thicken slightly as the eggs cook, but do not allow the mixture to get too hot or the eggs will curdle.

Quickly stir in the lemon rind and lemon juice, sprinkle with the parsley and serve.

Noodle hotpot with beef and tofu

500 g (1 lb 2 oz) rump steak, trimmed
  and thinly sliced
3 garlic cloves, crushed
2½ teaspoons sesame oil
60 ml (2 fl oz/¼ cup) soy sauce
80 ml (2½ fl oz/⅓ cup) Chinese rice wine
  or medium-sweet sherry
1 litre (35 fl oz/4 cups) chicken stock
6 dried chillies
6 cm (2½ inch) knob of fresh ginger,
  peeled and cut into thin matchsticks
175 g (6 oz) bean thread noodles
300 g (10½ oz/1 bunch) baby bok choy
  (pak choy), trimmed and chopped
½ Chinese cabbage, trimmed and sliced
100 g (3½ oz) fresh shiitake or oyster
  mushrooms, sliced
300 g (10½ oz) firm tofu, cut into 2.5 cm
  (1 inch) chunks
150 g (5½ oz/1⅔ cups) bean sprouts,
  tails trimmed
1 large handful coriander (cilantro) leaves
2 spring onions (scallions), thinly sliced
  on the diagonal
Chinese chilli sauce, to serve

Put the beef, garlic, sesame oil, 1½ tablespoons of the soy sauce and 1½ tablespoons of the rice wine in a large bowl. Toss well to coat the beef, then cover and set aside while making the broth.

Pour the stock and 1 litre (35 fl oz/4 cups) water into a large saucepan. Add the chillies, ginger and remaining soy sauce and rice wine and slowly bring to the boil. Add the noodles and simmer for 2 minutes, or until beginning to soften, then stir in the beef mixture and simmer for 1 minute, or until the beef is partly cooked.

Add the bok choy, cabbage, mushrooms and tofu and cook for 2 minutes, or until the vegetables have wilted, the tofu is warmed through and the beef is cooked.

Divide the mixture among warm large, deep bowls. Serve the bean sprouts, coriander and spring onion separately for scattering over the soup. Serve with Chinese chilli sauce.

Cambodian-style fish, tomato and pineapple soup

60 g (2¼ oz/¼ cup) tamarind pulp
2 lemongrass stems, trimmed
2½ tablespoons chopped palm sugar
   (jaggery)
60 ml (2 fl oz/¼ cup) fish sauce
1.5 litres (52 fl oz/6 cups) chicken stock
   or water
½ small ripe sweet pineapple, trimmed,
   cored and cut into small chunks
750 g (1 lb 10 oz) firm white fish fillets
   (such as ling, blue eye or snapper),
   trimmed and cut into 2 cm (¾ inch)
   chunks
4 small tomatoes (about 500 g/1 lb 2 oz
   in total), cut into 2 cm (¾ inch) chunks
   or thin wedges
300 g (10½ oz) sugarsnap peas,
   trimmed
2 spring onions (scallions), thinly sliced
1–2 small red chillies, thinly sliced
3 kaffir lime leaves, very thinly sliced
   (optional)
herbs such as mint, coriander (cilantro),
   Thai basil and Vietnamese mint,
   to serve
trimmed bean sprouts, to serve

Put the tamarind pulp in a small heatproof bowl and pour 375 ml (13 fl oz/1½ cups) boiling water over. Stir with a fork to loosen the tamarind and leave to soak for 15 minutes, or until the tamarind has softened. Push the mixture through a sieve into a very large saucepan or stockpot, discarding the solids.

Cut the lemongrass stems in half lengthways, then bruise them with the back of a large knife. Tie the lemongrass pieces into knots, or fold them into a loose bundle and secure with kitchen string. Add to the pan with the palm sugar, fish sauce and stock. Slowly bring to the boil, then cover, reduce the heat to medium–low and simmer for 10 minutes.

Add the pineapple, fish, tomatoes and sugarsnap peas. Bring to a gentle simmer and cook, covered, for 2 minutes, or until the pineapple and vegetables begin to soften and the fish is cooked through. Season to taste with freshly ground black pepper, then stir in the spring onion, chilli and lime leaves, if using.

Divide the soup among warm bowls and serve immediately, with the herbs and bean sprouts passed separately.

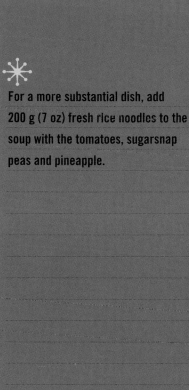

For a more substantial dish, add 200 g (7 oz) fresh rice noodles to the soup with the tomatoes, sugarsnap peas and pineapple.

Braised pork belly with daikon and greens

1.25 kg (2 lb 12 oz) piece of pork belly, with the skin still attached
1 tablespoon vegetable oil
2 star anise
1 cinnamon stick
2.5 cm (1 inch) knob of fresh ginger, peeled and cut into thin matchsticks
3 garlic cloves, peeled and bruised
125 ml (4 fl oz/½ cup) soy sauce
80 ml (2½ fl oz/⅓ cup) Chinese rice wine or sweet sherry
175 g (6 oz/¾ cup) chopped palm sugar (jaggery)
½ medium-sized daikon, peeled and cut into 2.5 cm (1 inch) chunks
4 baby bok choy (pak choy), trimmed and chopped
roasted unsalted peanuts, to serve (optional)

Cut the pork into 2.5 cm (1 inch) chunks. Place in a large heavy-based saucepan and cover with cold water. Slowly bring to a simmer, then cook over medium–low heat for 3–5 minutes. Drain the pork well and set aside.

Place the saucepan back over the heat and add the oil. Add the star anise, cinnamon stick, ginger and garlic and cook for 1 minute, or until fragrant.

Add the soy sauce, rice wine, palm sugar, pork and 500 ml (17 fl oz/2 cups) water. Stir to combine, then bring to a simmer, skimming off any froth that rises to the surface. Reduce the heat to low and cook, covered, for 30 minutes, skimming the surface often. Add the daikon, then cover and cook for a further 1 hour, or until the pork and daikon are tender.

Strain the mixture, reserving the broth. Return the broth to the pan, bring to the boil and cook for 10 minutes, or until reduced and thickened slightly. Return the pork mixture to the pan. Add the bok choy, then cover and cook for 1–2 minutes, or until the bok choy is tender and the meat and daikon are heated through.

Divide among warm bowls, scatter with peanuts if desired and serve.

Preparation time: 25 minutes   **Cooking time:** 2 hours   **Serves:** 6

Preparation time: 10 minutes ☀ **Cooking time:** 25 minutes ☀ **Serves:** 4

Creamy ricotta ravioli with silverbeet, nutmeg and lemon

500 g (1 lb 2 oz) fresh ricotta ravioli or ricotta tortellini

2½ tablespoons olive oil

1 small onion, finely chopped

1 garlic clove, crushed

400 g (14 oz/½ bunch) silverbeet (Swiss chard), stems removed, leaves washed, dried and thinly sliced

a large pinch of freshly grated nutmeg

250 ml (9 fl oz/1 cup) cream

2 tablespoons capers, rinsed and drained

2 tablespoons lemon juice

1 tomato, seeded and finely chopped

35 g (1¼ oz/⅓ cup) grated parmesan cheese

Bring a large saucepan of salted water to the boil. Add the pasta and cook according to the packet instructions until al dente. Drain the pasta, reserving the pan, and set the pasta aside in a bowl. Gently toss ½ tablespoon of the olive oil through the pasta to stop it sticking together.

Heat the remaining oil in the saucepan, add the onion and sauté over medium heat for 5 minutes, or until softened. Add the garlic, silverbeet and nutmeg and cook for a further 3–4 minutes, or until the silverbeet has wilted.

Pour in the cream, bring to the boil, then reduce the heat to a simmer and cook for 3–4 minutes, or until the liquid has reduced by half. Return the ravioli to the pan, add the capers and lemon juice and gently toss to combine well.

Season to taste with sea salt and freshly ground black pepper, scatter the chopped tomato and grated parmesan over and serve.

Chicken and black bean soup with avocado salsa

If you don't happen to have a lime handy, you can use lemon rind and juice in the avocado salsa. For a vegetarian version of this dish, omit the chicken and replace the chicken stock with vegetable stock.

2 tablespoons olive oil
8 chicken thigh fillets (about
  500 g/1 lb 2 oz), trimmed and cut into
  2 cm (¾ inch) chunks
1 onion, finely chopped
2 carrots, finely chopped
2 celery stalks, thinly sliced
1 red capsicum (pepper), cut into 1 cm
  (½ inch) pieces
1½ teaspoons ground cumin
½ teaspoon chilli powder, or to taste
1 teaspoon ground coriander
410 g (14½ oz) tin black beans, rinsed
  and drained
150 g (5½ oz/1 cup) frozen corn kernels
1 litre (35 fl oz/4 cups) chicken stock
400 g (14 oz) tin chopped tomatoes
125 g (4½ oz/½ cup) sour cream
2 large soft tortillas, warmed through
  and cut into thin strips

Avocado salsa

1 avocado, cut into 1 cm (½ inch)
  chunks
1 small handful coriander (cilantro)
  leaves, chopped
1 teaspoon finely grated lime rind
2 tablespoons lime juice

Heat the olive oil in a large heavy-based saucepan or casserole dish over medium heat. Add the chicken and cook, stirring often, for 5–6 minutes, or until golden all over. Remove to a plate and set aside.

Add the onion, carrot, celery and capsicum to the pan and sauté for 5 minutes, or until the onion starts to soften. Add the spices and cook for 1 minute, or until fragrant, stirring constantly. Return the chicken to the pan and add the beans, corn, stock and tomatoes. Bring to the boil, then reduce the heat to medium–low and simmer for 20 minutes, or until the chicken is tender.

For the avocado salsa, put all the ingredients in a small bowl and gently mix together.

Ladle the soup into warm deep bowls. Spoon a dollop of sour cream onto each. Top with a generous spoonful of the avocado salsa and the tortilla strips and serve.

Preparation time: 20 minutes   Cooking time: 35 minutes   Serves: 4–6

Preparation time: 10 minutes
plus 10 minutes soaking

Cooking time: 10 minutes

Serves: 4–6

Mee goreng

200 g (7 oz) dried thin egg noodles
60 ml (2 fl oz/¼ cup) vegetable oil
2 eggs, lightly beaten
2 garlic cloves, chopped
1 cm (½ inch) knob of fresh ginger,
  peeled and grated
1 carrot, cut into thin matchsticks
½ Chinese cabbage, cut into slices
  1 cm (½ inch) thick
60 ml (2 fl oz/¼ cup) soy sauce
2 tablespoons tomato sauce (ketchup)
1½ tablespoons chilli sauce, or to taste
8 fried tofu puffs, cut into quarters
100 g (3½ oz/1 cup) bean sprouts,
  tails trimmed
2 spring onions (scallions), sliced on
  the diagonal
sliced red chilli, to serve (optional)
lime wedges, to serve

Put the noodles in a large heatproof bowl and pour enough boiling water over to cover. Leave to soak for 10 minutes, or until the noodles are soft. Drain well.

Heat 1 tablespoon of the oil in a wok over medium–high heat. Add half the beaten egg and swirl the wok to spread it as thinly as possible. Cook for 1 minute, or until the egg has set and is golden underneath. Remove to a plate, then repeat with the remaining egg. Allow the omelettes to cool, then roll each one into a cylinder and slice thinly.

Reheat the wok over medium–high heat. Pour in the remaining oil. When the oil is hot, add the garlic, ginger, carrot and cabbage and stir-fry for 1 minute. Add the noodles and cook, tossing well, for another minute.

Add the soy sauce, tomato sauce and chilli sauce, tossing and cooking for another minute, or until the noodles are well coated and heated through. Add the omelette strips, tofu, bean sprouts and spring onion and toss to combine.

Sprinkle with sliced chilli, if desired, and serve with lime wedges.

Sweet and sour pork noodle stir-fry

You can vary the herbs in this dish — try Thai basil or Vietnamese mint instead of the coriander. Instead of the snow peas you could use trimmed sugarsnap peas, or green beans cut into 4 cm (1½ inch) lengths.

60 ml (2 fl oz/¼ cup) rice vinegar or white vinegar

1½ tablespoons soft brown sugar

2½ tablespoons soy sauce

2 teaspoons sesame oil

2 tablespoons vegetable oil

500 g (1 lb 2 oz) pork fillet, trimmed and cut into slices 5 mm (¼ inch) thick

6 spring onions (scallions), cut into 3 cm (1¼ inch) lengths

3 garlic cloves, finely chopped

1 tablespoon finely chopped fresh ginger

1 red capsicum (pepper), cut into strips 5 mm (¼ inch) wide

100 g (3½ oz) snow peas (mangetout), trimmed and cut in half on the diagonal

½ very ripe, small sweet pineapple, trimmed, cored and cut into 1.5 cm (⅝ inch) chunks (about 1 cup)

200 g (7 oz) crisp fried noodles (available from the Asian section of supermarkets)

2 tablespoons chopped coriander (cilantro) leaves, plus a few sprigs, to garnish

Put the vinegar, sugar, soy sauce and sesame oil in a bowl and mix well to dissolve the sugar. Set aside.

Heat 1½ tablespoons of the vegetable oil in a large wok until very hot. Add half the pork and cook, tossing the wok constantly, for 1–2 minutes, or until the pork has just changed colour. Remove to a plate using a slotted spoon. Reheat the wok if necessary, cook the remaining pork as before, then remove from the wok and set aside.

Heat the remaining oil in the wok. Add the spring onion, garlic and ginger and stir-fry over high heat for 2–3 seconds, taking care not to let the mixture burn.

Add the capsicum, snow peas and pineapple and stir-fry for 2–3 minutes, tossing occasionally, or until the vegetables have heated through and the capsicum has softened.

Add the soy sauce mixture and pork to the wok, toss to combine and bring just to the boil. Add the noodles and coriander and toss together well. Divide among warm deep bowls, scatter with the coriander sprigs and serve.

Preparation time: 20 minutes   **Cooking time:** 10 minutes   **Serves:** 4

Preparation time: 45 minutes
plus 2 hours marinating

Cooking time: 1 hour 15 minutes

Serves: 6

Beef and carrot stew with five-spice and star anise

2½ tablespoons chopped palm sugar (jaggery)

¼ teaspoon Chinese five-spice

60 ml (2 fl oz/¼ cup) fish sauce

1.25 kg (2 lb 12 oz) gravy beef or chuck steak, trimmed and cut into 4 cm (1½ inch) chunks

plain (all-purpose) flour, for dusting

60 ml (2 fl oz/¼ cup) peanut oil

2 large onions, sliced

4 garlic cloves, crushed

3 cm (1¼ inch) knob of fresh ginger, peeled and cut into thin matchsticks

3 carrots, sliced into 5 mm (¼ inch) rounds

60 g (2¼ oz/¼ cup) tomato paste (concentrated purée)

2 tablespoons soy sauce

2 star anise

1 cinnamon stick

6 small dried red chillies

1 lemongrass stem, trimmed and bruised

600 ml (21 fl oz) beef stock

6 baby bok choy (pak choy), ends trimmed and leaves separated

50 g (1¾ oz/⅓ cup) roasted peanuts (optional)

crusty baguette, to serve

Put the palm sugar, five-spice and 2 tablespoons of the fish sauce in a large bowl and stir to dissolve the sugar. Add the beef and toss to coat well, then cover and marinate in the refrigerator for 2 hours.

Drain the beef well, discarding the marinade. Lightly dust with the flour, shaking off the excess.

Heat the peanut oil in a large, heavy-based flameproof casserole dish or heavy-based saucepan to medium–high. Add the beef, onion, garlic and ginger and sauté for 5 minutes, or until the meat is sealed all over and the onion has softened. Add the carrot, remaining fish sauce, tomato paste, soy sauce, spices, lemongrass and stock.

Bring the mixture slowly to a simmer, skimming off any froth that rises to the surface. Cover and cook over low heat for 1 hour, or until the meat is tender.

Discard the lemongrass, then add the bok choy. Cover and simmer for 4 minutes, or until the bok choy is tender.

Divide the bok choy and stew among warm deep bowls, scatter with the peanuts, if using, and serve with a sliced crusty baguette.

Chicken risoni with orange and basil

20 g (¾ oz) unsalted butter

1 tablespoon olive oil

2 leeks, white part only, washed well, cut in half lengthways, then cut into 1 cm (½ inch) slices

500 g (1 lb 2 oz) chicken thigh fillets, trimmed and cut into 2 cm (¾ inch) chunks

60 ml (2 fl oz/¼ cup) white wine

500 ml (17 fl oz/2 cups) chicken stock

2 garlic cloves, finely chopped

1 tablespoon tomato paste (concentrated purée)

1 rosemary sprig

zest of ½ orange, cut into strips 1 cm (½ inch) wide, all white pith removed, plus 1 teaspoon finely grated orange rind

300 g (10½ oz/1½ cups) risoni (rice-shaped pasta)

2 zucchini (courgettes), cut into 5 mm (¼ inch) rounds

80 ml (2½ fl oz/⅓ cup) orange juice

1 handful basil leaves, torn

2 roma (plum) tomatoes, finely diced

shaved pecorino cheese, to serve

Heat the butter and oilve oil in a heavy-based saucepan over medium–low heat. Add the leek and sauté for 10 minutes, or until very soft. Remove to a plate and set aside.

Increase the heat to medium–high. Add the chicken to the pan and cook for 5 minutes, stirring occasionally.

Return the leek to the pan, then pour in the wine and cook for 1 minute, or until the liquid has reduced by half. Add the stock, garlic, tomato paste, rosemary sprig and orange zest and bring to the boil. Reduce the heat to medium and simmer for 7–8 minutes, or until the chicken is nearly tender. Season to taste with sea salt and freshly ground black pepper.

Stir in the risoni and 250 ml (9 fl oz/1 cup) boiling water, adding some extra boiling water if necessary to cover all the ingredients. Cover and simmer for 6 minutes, then add the zucchini and cook for another 2–3 minutes, or until the risoni and zucchini are just tender. The mixture should be a little sloppy.

Discard the rosemary sprig and orange zest. Stir in the grated orange rind, orange juice, basil and tomato. Divide among warm deep bowls, scatter with shaved pecorino and serve.

Preparation time: 15 minutes　　　**Cooking time:** 35 minutes　　　**Serves:** 4–6

Tofu, cashew and noodle stir-fry

300 g (10½ oz) fresh hokkien (egg)
  noodles or fresh rice noodles
1 teaspoon sesame oil
2 tablespoons soy sauce
60 ml (2 fl oz/¼ cup) oyster sauce
2 tablespoons vegetable oil
1 onion, thinly sliced
2 garlic cloves, thinly sliced
1 tablespoon finely grated fresh ginger
200 g (7 oz/1 bunch) broccolini, stems
  and heads halved lengthways, then
  cut into 5 cm (2 inch) lengths
300 g (10½ oz/1 bunch) bok choy
  (pak choy), trimmed and cut into 5 cm
  (2 inch) lengths
150 g (5½ oz) firm tofu, cut into 2 cm
  (¾ inch) chunks
100 g (3½ oz) snow peas (mangetout),
  cut in half on the diagonal
50 g (1¾ oz/⅓ cup) roasted cashew nuts

Put the noodles in a large heatproof bowl and pour in enough boiling water to cover. Leave to stand for 2–3 minutes, or until softened, then drain well.

In a small bowl, mix together the sesame oil, soy sauce, oyster sauce and 60 ml (2 fl oz/¼ cup) water. Set aside.

Heat the vegetable oil in a wok over high heat. Stir-fry the onion and garlic for 1 minute, then add the ginger, broccolini and bok choy and stir-fry for another minute.

Add the drained noodles, tofu and snow peas and stir-fry for 1–2 minutes, then add the soy sauce mixture and stir-fry for another 2–3 minutes, or until the liquid boils and the vegetables are tender but still slightly crisp.

Divide among warm bowls, scatter the cashews over and serve.

Fresh rice noodles are available from Asian food stores. You'll find hokkien noodles in Asian and regular supermarkets. This dish is very versatile — you could basically substitute any seasonal fresh vegetables here. Just adjust the cooking time slightly as required.

Beef pho

200 g (7 oz) sirloin steak, trimmed
1 cm (½ inch) knob of fresh ginger, peeled and thinly sliced
½ cinnamon stick, broken
2 star anise
2 cardamom pods, bruised
1 litre (35 fl oz/4 cups) beef stock
2 tablespoons fish sauce, or to taste
1½ tablespoons shaved palm sugar (jaggery)
750 g (1 lb 10 oz) fresh rice vermicelli noodles
2 handfuls coriander (cilantro) leaves
1 large handful Vietnamese mint (or regular mint)
100 g (3½ oz/1 cup) bean sprouts, tails trimmed
1 red chilli, seeded and thinly sliced
1 lime, cut into wedges
hoisin sauce, to serve

Place the steak in the freezer for 40–50 minutes, or until firm. Cut into slices 2 mm (1/16 inch) thick, place on a plate in a single layer and set aside.

Put the ginger, cinnamon, star anise and cardamom pods on a square of muslin (cheesecloth), then tie into a bundle, securing it well. Place in a saucepan and pour in the stock, then stir in the fish sauce and sugar. Bring to the boil, cover and reduce the heat to medium–low. Simmer for 10 minutes, or until the stock is aromatic. Remove the spice bundle and discard.

Meanwhile, place the noodles in a large heatproof bowl. Pour boiling water over to cover and leave to soak for 3–4 minutes, or until softened and warmed through. Drain well.

To serve, divide the noodles among large warm bowls. Arrange the beef slices on the noodles, then ladle the boiling stock over the top — the heat from the stock will be sufficient to cook the beef.

Serve the coriander, mint, bean sprouts, chilli, lime wedges and hoisin sauce separately for diners to flavour their soup.

Preparation time: 15 minutes
plus 50 minutes freezing

Cooking time: 15 minutes

Serves: 4

✳ **Preparation time:** 20 minutes   ✳ **Cooking time:** 35 minutes   ✳ **Serves:** 4

Mussel and sweet corn chowder

250 ml (9 fl oz/1 cup) white wine
500 ml (17 fl oz/2 cups) fish stock
1 bay leaf
1 kg (2 lb 4 oz) mussels, bearded
    and scrubbed
20 g (¾ oz) butter
1 tablespoon olive oil
1 leek, white part only, washed well
    and finely chopped
1 bacon slice, finely chopped
4 small waxy (boiling) potatoes (about
    400 g/14 oz in total), peeled and cut
    into 1.5 cm (⅝ inch) chunks
420 g (15 oz) tin corn kernels, drained
310 g (11 oz) tin creamed corn
125 ml (4 fl oz/½ cup) cream
3 tablespoons finely chopped parsley
toasted ciabatta or Turkish bread, to serve

Pour the wine and stock into a large heavy-based saucepan. Add the bay leaf and bring to the boil. Add the mussels, then cover and simmer for 3 minutes, or until the shells have just opened; discard any mussels that don't open. Transfer the mussels and the cooking liquid to a large bowl and set aside.

Wipe out the saucepan and place over medium–low heat. Add the butter and olive oil. When the butter has melted, add the leek, bacon and potato and sauté for 10 minutes, or until the leek is softened but not browned.

Strain the reserved mussel cooking liquid through a fine sieve into the pan. Increase the heat and simmer for 15 minutes, or until the potato is tender. Meanwhile, remove the mussel meat from the shells and set aside.

Stir the corn kernels, creamed corn and cream into the chowder. Bring to a low simmer and cook for 5 minutes, or until heated through. Stir in the mussel meat and half the parsley, then season to taste with freshly ground black pepper.

Ladle into warm deep bowls and scatter with the remaining parsley. Serve with toasted ciabatta or Turkish bread.

If you don't have any fish stock, use chicken or vegetable stock instead. You can often buy packets of prepared live mussels ready for the pot. Chowder is traditionally a thick hearty soup, but you can add a little more cream and/or stock to thin it out, if you prefer.

Pork and egg pad Thai

400 g (14 oz) fresh rice noodles
2 tablespoons peanut oil
200 g (7 oz) firm tofu, cut into 2 cm
 (¾ inch) chunks
2 garlic cloves, crushed
1 large pork fillet (about 400 g/14 oz),
 trimmed and very thinly sliced
2 eggs
125 g (4½ oz/½ cup) pad Thai paste
 (*see tip*)
1 tablespoon shaved palm sugar (jaggery)
2 tablespoons lime juice
80 g (2¾ oz/½ cup) chopped roasted
 peanuts
4 spring onions (scallions), sliced
100 g (3½ oz/1 cup) bean sprouts,
 tails trimmed
1 large handful coriander (cilantro) leaves
lemon wedges, to serve

Place the noodles in a large heatproof bowl. Pour in enough boiling water to cover, then leave to soak for 3–4 minutes, or until softened. Loosen with chopsticks or tongs, then drain well and set aside.

Meanwhile, heat half the oil in a wok over medium–high heat. Add the tofu and garlic and stir-fry for 2–3 minutes, or until golden. Remove with a slotted spoon and drain on paper towels.

Heat the remaining oil in the wok over high heat. Add the pork in batches and stir-fry for 4–5 minutes, or until the pork is just cooked, removing each batch to a bowl.

Lightly beat the eggs, then add to the wok and cook without stirring for 1–2 minutes, or until just set. Break the omelette up a bit, then return the tofu and the pork mixture to the wok. Add the noodles, pad Thai paste, palm sugar and lime juice and toss well to combine.

Remove the wok from the heat and toss the peanuts, spring onion, bean sprouts and coriander through. Divide among warm bowls and serve with lemon wedges.

Preparation time: 30 minutes   **Cooking time:** 15 minutes   **Serves:** 4

Beef borscht

2 tablespoons olive oil

500 g (1 lb 2 oz) gravy beef or oyster blade, trimmed and cut into 2.5 cm (1 inch) chunks

2 onions, finely chopped

1 garlic clove, finely chopped

1 celery stalk, finely chopped

2 beetroot (beets), scrubbed, trimmed and cut in half

2 potatoes (500 g/1 lb 2 oz in total), peeled and cut into 1 cm (½ inch) chunks

2 carrots, coarsely grated

¼ savoy cabbage (about 300 g/10½ oz), core removed, then finely shredded

1 tablespoon chopped flat-leaf (Italian) parsley

1 bay leaf

1 teaspoon dill seeds

½ teaspoon celery seeds

500 ml (17 fl oz/2 cups) beef stock

2 tablespoons lemon juice, or to taste

3 tablespoons chopped dill

125 g (4½ oz/½ cup) sour cream

4 slices dark rye bread, toasted

Heat the olive oil in a large heavy-based saucepan over medium–high heat. Add the beef in batches and cook for 3 minutes, turning often, or until browned. Remove each batch to a plate and set aside.

Add the onion, garlic and celery to the pan and sauté for 5 minutes, or until softened. Stir in the beetroot, potato, carrot and cabbage. Return the beef to the saucepan and add the parsley, bay leaf, dill seeds and celery seeds. Pour in the stock and 1.5 litres (52 fl oz/6 cups) water and bring to the boil, then reduce the heat to low and simmer for 30–45 minutes, or until the vegetables and beef are very tender.

Remove and discard the bay leaf. Scoop out the beetroot halves and leave until cool enough to handle, then peel off the skin. Grate the beetroot and stir into the soup. Season to taste with sea salt and freshly ground black pepper, then stir in the lemon juice.

Mix 1 tablespoon of the dill through the sour cream, then spread over the toasted bread slices.

Ladle the soup into warm bowls, garnish with the remaining dill and serve with the toast slices.

Pumpernickel bread — a dark, heavy rye bread originally from Germany — is also delicious with this soup. When peeling the cooked beetroot, it's a good idea to wear gloves so your hands don't become stained.

Steamed Cantonese chicken with ginger and snow peas

4 small chicken breast fillets (about 600 g/1 lb 5 oz in total), cut on the diagonal into slices 2 cm (¾ inch) thick

1½ teaspoons cornflour (cornstarch)

1 garlic clove, chopped

2 cm (¾ inch) knob of fresh ginger, peeled and cut into thin matchsticks

a pinch of Chinese five-spice, or to taste

1 tablespoon oyster sauce

2 teaspoons soy sauce, plus extra, to serve

1 tablespoon hoisin sauce, plus extra, to serve

6 dried shiitake mushrooms

2 spring onions (scallions), cut into 2 cm (¾ inch) lengths

100 g (3½ oz) snow peas (mangetout), thinly sliced lengthways

4 baby bok choy (pak choy), trimmed, leaves halved lengthways

400 g (14 oz) fresh rice noodles

Put the chicken in a bowl with the cornflour, garlic, ginger, five-spice, oyster sauce, soy sauce and hoisin sauce. Toss well to coat the chicken, then cover and marinate in the refrigerator or at cool room temperature for 30 minutes.

Meanwhile, put the mushrooms in a small heatproof bowl and pour in enough boiling water to just cover. Allow to soak for 20 minutes, or until softened. Drain well, then cut off and discard the stems. Thinly slice the mushrooms and set aside.

Place the chicken mixture in a dish that will fit inside a large steamer and can hold all the chicken in a single layer. Place the mushrooms on top of the chicken. Bring some water to the boil in the base of the steamer, then place the chicken dish in and cover the steamer (the dish the chicken is sitting in shouldn't touch the water in the steamer). Cook for 10 minutes, then place the spring onion, snow peas and bok choy over the chicken. Cover and steam for 5 minutes, or until the vegetables are tender and the chicken is cooked through.

Meanwhile, place the noodles in a heatproof bowl, pour in enough boiling water to cover and leave to soak for 2–3 minutes, or until softened. Loosen the noodles with chopsticks or tongs, then drain well.

Divide the noodles among warm bowls and top with the vegetables and chicken. Serve with extra soy sauce and hoisin sauce for drizzling over.

✳ **Preparation time:** 15 minutes
plus 30 minutes marinating

✳ **Cooking time:** 20 minutes

✳ **Serves:** 4

Preparation time: 20 minutes   **Cooking time:** 15 minutes   **Serves:** 4–6

Chicken liver and mushroom sauté with spinach and cream

500 g (1 lb 2 oz) chicken livers, trimmed
1½ tablespoons olive oil
20 g (¾ oz) butter
1 large onion, halved and thinly sliced
2 garlic cloves, crushed
1 tablespoon chopped thyme
350 g (12 oz) button mushrooms, halved
250 ml (9 fl oz/1 cup) cream
200 g (7 oz) baby spinach leaves
2 tablespoons balsamic vinegar
crusty bread or toast, to serve

Cut the chicken livers in half and pat dry with paper towels.

Heat the olive oil and butter in a large frying pan over medium heat until the butter melts. Add the chicken livers and cook, turning often, for 3–4 minutes, or until browned but still pink on the inside — take care not to overcook them or they will be dry and tough. Remove to a plate using a slotted spoon and set aside.

Add the onion, garlic and thyme to the pan and sauté over low heat for 5 minutes, or until the onion has softened. Increase the heat to medium, then add the mushrooms and sauté for 3–4 minutes, or until they release their juices. Pour in the cream and bring to the boil.

Add the spinach and stir until the leaves wilt. Return the chicken livers to the pan and heat through. Stir in the vinegar, season with sea salt and freshly ground black pepper and serve on or with crusty bread or toast.

Instead of baby English spinach leaves you can use the larger variety. Wash and dry the leaves well and tear into bite-sized pieces.

Harira

Harira is a hearty, spicy soup from Morocco, where it is something of a national dish. It is mostly associated with the fasting month of Ramadan, when it is served to break the fast at the end of the day. There are various versions, but it popularly contains lamb, chickpeas, lentils, tomatoes and spices.

1 tablespoon olive oil
1 large red onion, finely chopped
400 g (14 oz) lamb neck or shoulder, trimmed and cut into 2 cm (¾ inch) chunks
½ cinnamon stick
1 teaspoon ground cumin
2 teaspoons sweet paprika
a pinch of saffron threads
500 ml (17 fl oz/2 cups) chicken stock
2 x 400 g (14 oz) tins chopped tomatoes
95 g (3¼ oz/½ cup) brown lentils
1 small handful chopped coriander (cilantro) leaves
2 tablespoons fine semolina
400 g (14 oz) tin chickpeas, rinsed and drained
60 ml (2 fl oz/¼ cup) lemon juice
lemon wedges, to serve

Heat the olive oil in a large heavy-based saucepan or casserole dish over medium–high heat. Add the onion and sauté for 5 minutes, or until softened. Add the lamb in batches and cook for 2–3 minutes, or until browned all over, removing each batch to a plate.

Reduce the heat to medium. Return all the lamb to the saucepan, then add the cinnamon stick, cumin, paprika, saffron and freshly ground black pepper to taste. Cook, stirring, for 1 minute, or until fragrant. Add the stock, tomatoes, lentils and half the coriander, then pour in 500 ml (17 fl oz/2 cups) water and bring to the boil. Reduce the heat to low and simmer for 1 hour, or until the lamb and lentils are tender, adding a little extra water if necessary to keep all the ingredients just covered.

In a small bowl, mix the semolina with 125 ml (4 fl oz/½ cup) cold water to form a smooth paste. Stir it into the soup, then add the chickpeas and simmer for 15 minutes, or until the soup has thickened slightly, stirring often to prevent lumps forming. Stir in the lemon juice and season to taste with sea salt.

Ladle the soup into warm bowls, scatter with the remaining coriander and serve with lemon wedges.

Preparation time: 20 minutes   **Cooking time:** 1 hour 30 minutes   **Serves:** 4

Preparation time: 15 minutes **Cooking time:** 15 minutes **Serves:** 4

Satay chicken noodles

250 g (9 oz) fresh rice noodles
400 ml (14 fl oz) tin coconut milk
60 g (2¼ oz/¼ cup) crunchy peanut
  butter
2 teaspoons soft brown sugar
1 tablespoon lime juice
2 tablespoons fish sauce
2 tablespoons peanut oil
500 g (1 lb 2 oz) chicken breast fillets,
  thinly sliced on the diagonal
60 g (2¼ oz/¼ cup) Thai Penang curry
  paste (see tip)
2 garlic cloves, chopped
1 red capsicum (pepper), thinly sliced
150 g (5½ oz) snow peas (mangetout),
  trimmed and cut on the diagonal
2 kaffir lime leaves, finely shredded
2 tablespoons coriander (cilantro) leaves
40 g (1½ oz/¼ cup) unsalted roasted
  peanuts, chopped

Put the noodles in a large heatproof bowl. Pour in enough boiling water to cover, then leave to soak for 3 minutes, or until soft. Drain well and set aside.

Meanwhile, put the coconut milk, peanut butter, sugar, lime juice and fish sauce in a small food processor and blend until a smooth paste forms. Set aside.

Heat 1½ tablespoons of the oil in a large wok over high heat. Add the chicken, curry paste and garlic in two batches. Stir-fry each batch for 2 minutes, or until the chicken is nearly cooked, removing each batch to a plate.

Reheat the wok and add the remaining oil. Stir-fry the capsicum over medium–high heat for 2 minutes, or until softened slightly. Add the peanut butter mixture and bring to a simmer. Return the chicken mixture to the wok, along with the snow peas. Toss for 1–2 minutes to heat the chicken through and soften the snow peas slightly.

Add the noodles and toss for another 1–2 minutes to heat through. Divide the mixture among warm bowls, scatter the lime leaves, coriander and peanuts over each and serve.

This is a very adaptable recipe. You can easily make this a vegetarian dish by using tofu instead of the chicken and adding more vegetables — or try a seafood version using prawns (shrimp).
Thai Penang curry is available from the Asian section in supermarkets.

Pork and noodles in lemongrass broth

1 orange sweet potato, peeled and cut
   into 1 cm (½ inch) chunks
300 g (10½ oz) pumpkin (winter squash),
   peeled and cut into 3 cm (1¼ inch)
   chunks
500 g (1 lb 2 oz) pork fillets, trimmed
   and sliced 5 mm (¼ inch) thick
250 g (7 oz) fresh rice noodles
65 g (2½ oz/¾ cup) bean sprouts,
   tails trimmed
1 handful coriander (cilantro) leaves
1 small handful mint leaves, torn
chilli sauce, to serve

Lemongrass broth

1 onion, sliced
2 lemongrass stems, trimmed and
   roughly chopped
1 green chilli, halved lengthways
5 cm (2 inch) knob of fresh ginger,
   peeled and sliced
2 garlic cloves, gently bruised
2 tablespoons coriander (cilantro) stems,
   roughly chopped
3 kaffir lime leaves, torn
60 ml (2 fl oz/¼ cup) fish sauce
2½ teaspoons grated palm sugar (jaggery)
2 litres (70 fl oz/8 cups) chicken stock

For the lemongrass broth, put the ingredients in a large saucepan over medium heat. Bring to the boil, then reduce the heat to medium–low and simmer for 10 minutes. Strain the broth, discarding the solids, and return to the pan.

Add the sweet potato and pumpkin to the lemongrass broth and simmer for 15 minutes, or until tender. Add the pork and noodles and simmer for 3 minutes, or until the pork is cooked through.

Ladle the soup into warm bowls and scatter with the bean sprouts, coriander and mint. Serve immediately, with chilli sauce passed separately.

Preparation time: 20 minutes   **Cooking time:** 35 minutes   **Serves:** 4–6

Preparation time: 15 minutes   Cooking time: 45 minutes   Serves: 6

Salmon with braised pumpkin and sesame cream

60 ml (2 fl oz/¼ cup) olive oil

2 onions, halved and sliced

2 large garlic cloves, crushed

1½ tablespoons finely chopped fresh ginger

4 cardamom pods, bruised

1 teaspoon ground turmeric

600 g (1 lb 5 oz) pumpkin (winter squash), peeled and cut into 2.5 cm (1 inch) chunks

2 x 400 g (14 oz) tins chopped tomatoes

400 g (14 oz) tin chickpeas, rinsed and drained

6 x 180 g (6 oz) skinless salmon or other firm fish fillets, bones removed

1 small handful coriander (cilantro) leaves

1½ tablespoons toasted sesame seeds (optional)

Sesame cream

125 g (4½ oz/½ cup) Greek-style yoghurt

1 tablespoon tahini

1 garlic clove, crushed

2 teaspoons lemon juice, or to taste

For the seame cream, put the ingredients in a small bowl, mix together well and season to taste with sea salt and freshly ground black pepper. Cover with plastic wrap and refrigerate until needed.

Heat the olive oil in a very large heavy-based saucepan or flameproof casserole dish over medium–low heat. Add the onion and sauté for 8–10 minutes, or until the onion is soft and starting to brown. Add the garlic, ginger, cardamom, turmeric and pumpkin and sauté for 2–3 minutes, or until fragrant.

Add the tomatoes and bring the mixture to a simmer. Cover, reduce the heat to low and cook for 15–20 minutes, or until the pumpkin is nearly tender, stirring occasionally. Season to taste, then stir in the chickpeas.

Place the salmon in a single layer over the vegetable mixture. Cover and cook for another 10–12 minutes, or until the salmon is cooked through but still a little pink in the middle.

Divide the mixture among warm plates and top each with a spoonful of sesame cream. Serve sprinkled with the coriander, and the sesame seeds if desired.

Lamb, lemon and barley soup

4 lamb shanks (about 1.75 kg/3 lb 13 oz in total), trimmed of fat
2 tablespoons extra virgin olive oil
2 leeks, white part only, washed well and finely chopped
2 celery stalks, cut into 1 cm (½ inch) lengths
2 garlic cloves, finely chopped
3 thyme sprigs
110 g (3¾ oz/½ cup) pearl barley
⅓ small cauliflower, cut into 5 mm (¼ inch) pieces (about 250 g/ 9 oz/2 cups)
2 zucchini (courgettes), sliced into 5 mm (¼ inch) rounds
400 g (14 oz) tin white beans, rinsed and drained
50 ml (1½ fl oz) lemon juice
1 teaspoon finely grated lemon rind
1 large handful mint
finely grated parmesan cheese, to serve (optional)

Put the shanks in a large heavy-based saucepan. Pour in 1.5 litres (52 fl oz/6 cups) water, or enough to cover the shanks. Bring just to the boil, then reduce the heat to low. Cover and simmer for 2 hours, or until the shanks are very tender, skimming the froth from the surface occasionally. Lift the shanks out and leave to cool. Transfer the stock to a large bowl, skim off any fat from the surface, then add enough water to make 2 litres (70 fl oz/8 cups) of liquid and reserve.

Heat the olive oil in the same saucepan over medium heat. Add the leek, celery and garlic and sauté for 5–6 minutes, or until starting to soften. Add the thyme sprigs, barley and reserved liquid and bring just to the boil. Reduce the heat to low, then simmer for 20 minutes, or until the barley is nearly tender.

Add the cauliflower and cook for 4 minutes, or until nearly tender, then add the zucchini and beans. Cook for 3–4 minutes, or until the vegetables are tender and cooked through. Meanwhile, remove the lamb from the bones and chop into 1 cm (½ inch) chunks.

Stir the lamb into the soup with the lemon juice and lemon rind. Season to taste with sea salt and freshly ground black pepper and divide among warm bowls. Serve sprinkled with mint and finely grated parmesan if desired.

Preparation time: 25 minutes   **Cooking time:** 2 hours 40 minutes   **Serves:** 4–6

Baked

Roast lamb with summer vegetables • Chicken with green rice and corn • Ham, ricotta and spinach cannelloni • Rice baked with beans, spinach, prawns and feta • Braised beef with horseradish dumplings • Lamb and carrot kuku • Stuffed fish on baked tomatoes and onion • Ricotta, provolone and salami pie • Cider-braised pork neck • Lamb chops with rosemary and almonds • Roast beef with mustard, beer and parsnips • Mexican chicken bake • Fish baked in paper • Sausages baked with potato and fennel • Deep-dish pizza • Falso magro • Beef bourguignon with garlic toasts • Swedish spinach meatballs • Baked fish with potato and fennel gratin • Lamb bobotie • Bread bake with salami, spinach and gruyère • Lamb and broad bean hotpot with polenta dumplings • Vegetable biryani with cumin pastry • Chicken with pine nut, caper and currant stuffing • Roast pork with apples, pumpkin and chestnut gravy • Turkey polpettoni with capsicum and olive sauce • Baked Spanish omelette • Baked chicken, pea and prosciutto risotto • Capsicums stuffed with lamb and couscous • Simple cassoulet • Tomato, bacon and egg lasagne • Baked tuna and cauliflower frittata • Ham baked beans with cheesy cornbread crust • Roast chicken with brussels sprouts, bacon and chestnuts • Root vegetable bake with crunchy cheesy almond crumbs • Chicken, mushroom and tarragon pot pie • Lamb, carrot and zucchini moussaka • Baked stuffed meatloaf • Lamb steaks baked with tomato, lentils, mint and feta • Pork and chorizo pie

Preparation time: 30 minutes   **Cooking time:** 1 hour 40 minutes   **Serves:** 6

Roast lamb with summer vegetables

1.5 kg (3 lb 5 oz) boneless leg of lamb
1 tablespoon capers, drained and
   roughly chopped
1 large handful parsley, finely chopped
6 anchovy fillets, chopped
2 garlic cloves, crushed
3 teaspoons lemon juice
½ teaspoon finely grated lemon rind
1 tablespoon olive oil

Summer vegetables

1 red onion, cut into 2 cm (¾ inch)
   chunks
1 red capsicum (pepper), cut into
   3 cm (1¼ inch) pieces
12 garlic cloves, peeled
1 eggplant (aubergine), cut into 2 cm
   (¾ inch) chunks
2 zucchini (courgettes), cut in half
   lengthways, then sliced
500 g (1 lb 2 oz) cherry tomatoes, halved
60 ml (2 fl oz/¼ cup) olive oil
1 small handful mint
50 g (1¾ oz/½ cup) shaved parmesan
   cheese

Preheat the oven to 180°C (350°F/Gas 4).

Remove any string or netting from the lamb, then open the lamb up, skin side down, on a chopping board. In a bowl mix together the capers, parsley, anchovies, garlic, lemon juice, lemon rind and olive oil. Spread the mixture over the lamb, reserving the bowl, then roll the lamb up and tie at 2 cm (¾ inch) intervals with kitchen string to keep it in a neat shape.

Place the lamb in a roasting tin and season with sea salt and freshly ground black pepper. Roast for 30 minutes.

Meanwhile, start preparing the summer vegetables. Put the onion, capsicum, garlic, eggplant, zucchini, tomatoes and olive oil in the reserved bowl. Season generously and toss to combine well.

Add the vegetable mixture to the roasting tin and bake for 45 minutes, or until the lamb is cooked to your liking and the vegetables have softened.

Remove the lamb to a plate, cover loosely with foil and allow to rest for 15 minutes. Meanwhile, roast the vegetables for a further 10 minutes, or until very tender. Transfer the vegetables to a serving bowl and scatter with the mint and shaved parmesan.

Carve the lamb in slices and serve with the summer vegetables.

Chicken with green rice and corn

60 ml (2 fl oz/¼ cup) extra virgin
  olive oil
2 onions, finely chopped
1 green capsicum (pepper), finely
  chopped
2 garlic cloves, finely chopped
1½ teaspoons cumin seeds
2 teaspoons dried oregano
8 chicken drumsticks, skin left on,
  knuckle end trimmed (ask your
  butcher to do this)
300 g (10½ oz/1½ cups) long-grain
  white rice
375 ml (13 fl oz/1½ cups) chicken
  stock or water
420 g (15 oz) tin corn kernels, drained
lime wedges, to serve

Spice paste
1 large green chilli, roughly chopped
150 g (5½ oz/3⅓ cups) baby English
  spinach leaves
1 large handful coriander (cilantro),
  roughly chopped
1 small handful flat-leaf (Italian) parsley,
  roughly chopped
finely grated rind and juice of 1 lime

Preheat the oven to 180°C (350°F/Gas 4).

Heat the olive oil in a large flameproof casserole dish over medium heat. Add the onion, capsicum and garlic and sauté for 6–7 minutes, or until softened. Stir in the cumin seeds and oregano until well combined, then remove the mixture to a bowl.

Add the chicken to the pan, in batches if necessary, and season with sea salt and freshly ground black pepper. Cook, turning often, for 3–4 minutes, or until sealed all over. Add the rice, stock, corn and onion mixture to the pan. Stir together well, then bring to the boil. Cover, transfer to the oven and bake for 25 minutes, or until the rice is nearly tender and the liquid is mostly absorbed.

Meanwhile, put the spice paste ingredients in a food processor and blend until a coarse paste forms. Stir it through the rice, then cover and bake for another 5 minutes, or until the mixture is heated through and the rice is tender. Serve with lime wedges.

Preparation time: 20 minutes **Cooking time:** 45 minutes **Serves:** 4–6

Preparation time: 25 minutes Cooking time: 35 minutes Serves: 6

Ham, ricotta and spinach cannelloni

250 g (9 oz) packet frozen spinach,
  thawed
400 g (14 oz/1⅔ cups) firm fresh
  ricotta cheese
100 g (3½ oz/1 cup) finely grated
  parmesan cheese
200 g (7 oz) leg ham off the bone,
  finely chopped
2 egg yolks
1 garlic clove, crushed
50 g (1¾ oz/⅓ cup) pine nuts, chopped
2 tablespoons chopped basil, plus extra,
  to garnish
ground white pepper, to taste
20 instant dried cannelloni shells
  (about 230 g/8 oz)
375 ml (13 fl oz/1½ cups) cream
2½ tablespoons chicken stock
a pinch of freshly grated nutmeg
halved cherry tomatoes, to garnish

Preheat the oven to 180°C (350°F/Gas 4).

Place the spinach in a clean tea towel (dish towel) and squeeze firmly to remove as much water as possible. Finely chop the spinach and place in a bowl with the ricotta, half the parmesan, the ham, egg yolks, garlic, pine nuts and basil. Season with sea salt and ground white pepper and mix together well.

Spoon the filling into the cannelloni shells, then arrange in a 20 x 32 cm (8 x 13 inch) baking dish (or one of 3.5 litre/122 fl oz/14 cup capacity).

Mix together the cream, stock and half the remaining parmesan and season to taste. Pour over the cannelloni and sprinkle with the remaining parmesan and nutmeg.

Cover with foil and bake for 20 minutes, then remove the foil and bake for a further 15 minutes, or until the top is golden and the sauce is bubbling. Serve hot, garnished with cherry tomatoes and basil.

Rice baked with beans, spinach, prawns and feta

1 tablespoon olive oil
1 red onion, finely chopped
2 garlic cloves, crushed
½ teaspoon chilli flakes, or to taste
2 teaspoons thyme leaves
300 g (10½ oz/1½ cups) long-grain white rice
560 ml (19¼ fl oz/2¼ cups) vegetable or chicken stock
400 g (14 oz) tin cannellini beans, rinsed and drained
175 g (6 oz/1 cup) fresh or thawed frozen broad (fava) beans, peeled
250 g (9 oz) packet frozen chopped spinach, thawed and squeezed dry
500 g (1 lb 2 oz) raw king prawns (shrimp), peeled and deveined, tails intact
150 g (5½ oz/1 cup) crumbled feta cheese
lemon wedges, to serve

Preheat the oven to 180°C (350°F/Gas 4).

Heat the olive oil in a 3 litre (105 fl oz/12 cup) flameproof casserole dish over medium heat. Add the onion and sauté for 5 minutes, or until softened. Add the garlic, chilli flakes and thyme and sauté for 1 minute, or until fragrant. Add the rice and stir until well coated with the oil.

Stir in the stock and season well with freshly ground black pepper, mixing thoroughly to combine. Bring to a simmer, then cover the dish, transfer to the oven and bake for 30 minutes, or until the rice is tender and the liquid is absorbed.

Add the cannellini beans, broad beans, spinach and prawns, pushing them into the rice so that they are covered. Scatter the feta over the top, then cover and bake for a further 10 minutes, or until the vegetables and prawns are cooked.

Fluff up the rice with a fork. Serve hot, with lemon wedges.

Preparation time: 15 minutes   **Cooking time:** 50 minutes   **Serves:** 4

Preparation time: 45 minutes   **Cooking time:** 2 hours   **Serves:** 4

Braised beef with horseradish dumplings

1.4 kg (3 lb 2 oz) chuck or other
  braising steak, cut into 3 cm (1¼ inch)
  chunks
35 g (1¼ oz/¼ cup) plain (all-purpose)
  flour
60 ml (2 fl oz/¼ cup) olive oil
2 onions, finely chopped
100 g (3½ oz) speck or smoked bacon,
  finely chopped
2 teaspoons caraway seeds
2 kohlrabi (about 500 g/1 lb 2 oz
  in total), peeled and cut into 2 cm
  (¾ inch) chunks
2 granny smith apples, peeled, cored
  and quartered, then cut into 2 cm
  (¾ inch) chunks
250 ml (9 fl oz/1 cup) sweet alcoholic
  apple cider
500 ml (17 fl oz/2 cups) beef stock
2 thyme sprigs
chopped flat-leaf (Italian) parsley,
  to serve

Horseradish dumplings

3 desiree potatoes (about 400 g/14 oz
  in total), peeled and cut into 5 mm
  (¼ inch) slices
2 eggs, lightly beaten
60 g (2¼ oz/¼ cup) horseradish cream
1 small handful flat-leaf (Italian) parsley,
  finely chopped
150 g (5½ oz/1 cup) self-raising flour,
  sifted

Preheat the oven to 170°C (325°F/Gas 3).

To make the horseradish dumplings, bring some salted water to the boil in a large flameproof casserole dish, add the potato slices and cook for 7–8 minutes, or until tender. Drain well, reserving the dish, and place the slices in a bowl to cool slightly. Add the eggs, horseradish cream and parsley to the potato and season well with sea salt and freshly ground black pepper. Stir with a wooden spoon or mash with a fork until the mixture is smooth and comes together. Cover and set aside.

Toss the beef in the flour to coat, shaking off any excess. Season the meat well. Heat 1 tablespoon of the olive oil in the casserole dish over medium heat. Sauté the onion, speck and caraway seeds for 7–8 minutes, or until the onion has softened. Remove to a large bowl. Heat another tablespoon of oil in the dish, then add half the beef and cook over medium–high heat for 4–5 minutes, turning often, or until browned all over. Add to the onion mixture. Heat the remaining oil in the dish and brown the remaining beef.

Return the onion and beef mixtures to the dish. Add the kohlrabi, apple, cider, stock and thyme sprigs and slowly bring to a simmer. Cover, transfer to the oven and bake for 50 minutes.

Add the flour to the dumpling mixture and combine well. Turn out onto a lightly floured surface, then form into two logs about 30 cm (12 inches) long. Cut each log into 10 rounds about 3 cm (1¼ inches) thick, then roll each piece into a ball. Place the dumplings on top of the braise, then cover and bake for 20 minutes. Remove the lid and bake for another 20 minutes, or until the dumplings are cooked.

Divide the braise and dumplings among warm deep bowls, scatter with parsley and serve.

Lamb and carrot kuku

1 tablespoon olive oil
1 onion, finely diced
300 g (10½ oz) minced (ground) lamb
½ teaspoon ground cumin
½ teaspoon ground cinnamon
a pinch of saffron threads
1 large carrot, roughly grated
1 handful coriander (cilantro) leaves,
  roughly chopped
1 small handful mint, roughly chopped,
  plus extra, to garnish
6 eggs, lightly beaten
yoghurt, to serve

Preheat the oven to 160°C (315°F/Gas 2–3).

Heat the olive oil in an 18 cm (7 inch) ovenproof non-stick frying pan over medium heat. Add the onion and sauté for 2 minutes, or until starting to soften. Add the lamb and cook for 5 minutes, or until golden, breaking up the lumps with a wooden spoon. Add the cumin, cinnamon and saffron and cook, stirring, for 1 minute, or until fragrant.

Remove from the heat and stir the carrot, coriander and mint through. Return to the heat, then pour in the eggs and cook for 3 minutes, or until the edge of the omelette begins to turn golden brown. Transfer the pan to the oven and bake for 20 minutes, or until the omelette is firm to the touch.

Cut the omelette into wedges, sprinkle with mint and serve with a spoonful of yoghurt.

Preparation time: 10 minutes   **Cooking time:** 35 minutes   **Serves:** 4

Preparation time: 30 minutes   **Cooking time:** 55 minutes   **Serves:** 4–6

Stuffed fish on baked tomatoes and onion

2 large red potatoes, peeled and halved, then cut into slices 1 cm (½ inch) thick

5 roma (plum) tomatoes, roughly chopped

2 small red onions, thinly sliced

250 ml (9 fl oz/1 cup) white wine

2 kg (4 lb 8 oz) whole snapper or similar white fish, scaled and gutted

3 spring onions (scallions), thinly sliced

1 garlic clove, crushed

30 g (1 oz/¼ cup) walnuts, roughly chopped

1 tablespoon pomegranate molasses

1 tablespoon lemon juice

1 teaspoon finely grated lemon rind

75 g (2½ oz/½ cup) currants

50 g (1¾ oz/½ cup) breadcrumbs, made from day-old bread

1 small handful chopped flat-leaf (Italian) parsley, chopped

2 tablespoons chopped coriander (cilantro) leaves

2 tablespoons chopped mint

2½ tablespoons olive oil

lemon wedges, to serve

Preheat the oven to 200°C (400°F/Gas 6).

Put the potato, tomato, onion and wine in a baking dish large enough to hold the fish. Toss to combine, then cover with foil and bake for 15 minutes.

Place the fish on a large board. Using a sharp knife, cut three slits into each side of the fish, near the head. Put the spring onion, garlic, walnuts, pomegranate molasses, lemon juice, lemon rind, currants, breadcrumbs and herbs in a bowl. Mix together, then place in the cavity of the fish.

Remove the foil from the baking dish and place the fish over the tomato mixture. Drizzle the fish with the olive oil and bake for 35–40 minutes, or until the flesh is firm to the touch and cooked through.

Serve the fish with the baked tomato mixture and lemon wedges.

This recipe would also work well using 4 small fish, so each diner gets one each; baby snapper, whiting, river trout or bream would all be good. Reduce the cooking time to 15–20 minutes. To check if the fish is cooked, use a small sharp knife to see if the flesh flakes easily down to the bone through the thickest part of the fish (usually the very middle of each side).

Ricotta, provolone and salami pie

2 sheets frozen shortcrust pastry (each 25 cm/10 inches square), thawed
2 egg yolks, beaten with 1 tablespoon cold water, for glazing
250 g (9 oz) packet frozen spinach, thawed
500 g (1 lb 2 oz/2 cups) firm fresh ricotta cheese
2 eggs, lightly beaten
155 g (5½ oz/1 cup) chopped smoked cooked ham
100 g (3½ oz) chopped mild Italian salami
100 g (3½ oz) thinly sliced pancetta, chopped
110 g (3¾ oz/¾ cup) chopped provolone cheese
50 g (1¾ oz/½ cup) grated parmesan cheese
1 small handful flat-leaf (Italian) parsley, finely chopped

Preheat the oven to 200°C (400°F/Gas 6).

Grease a pie dish that is about 4 cm (1½ inches) deep, with a 23 cm (9 inch) base and 25 cm (10 inch) top.

Place one sheet of pastry in the pie dish, easing it in to cover the base and side. Trim the edges, using the scraps to patch up any gaps if necessary. Place a sheet of baking paper over the pastry, then fill with baking beads or dried beans. Bake for 12 minutes.

Reduce the oven temperature to 180°C (350°F/Gas 4). Remove the beans and baking paper, then brush the pastry all over with some of the egg yolk mixture. Bake for another 8 minutes, or until the pastry is dry to the touch. Remove from the oven.

Meanwhile, place the spinach in a colander and press firmly to extract as much liquid as possible. Place the spinach in a clean tea towel (dish towel), then wring out all the remaining liquid; the spinach should be quite dry. Place in a bowl with the remaining ingredients. Mix together well, then season with freshly ground black pepper.

Brush a little of the remaining yolk mixture over the edge of the baked pastry base. Spread the filling over the pastry base, smoothing the surface even. Cover the filling with the remaining sheet of pastry, trimming the edges and pressing them to seal, and patching up any gaps with any pastry trimmings if necessary. Brush the top with the remaining egg yolk mixture, then make a few slits using a small sharp knife, to allow steam to escape. Bake for 30 minutes, or until the pastry is golden. Serve hot or cold.

Preparation time: 20 minutes　　**Cooking time:** 50 minutes　　**Serves:** 6

Preparation time: 20 minutes　**Cooking time:** 2 hours 45 minutes　**Serves:** 4–6

Cider-braised pork neck

1.25 kg (2 lb 12 oz) pork neck, trimmed
olive oil, for brushing and pan-frying
1½ teaspoons ground cinnamon
1½ teaspoons ground cumin
1 onion, finely chopped
1 celery stalk, finely chopped
2 garlic cloves, crushed
2 thyme sprigs
500 ml (17 fl oz/2 cups) sweet alcoholic
    apple cider
1 orange sweet potato (about 425 g/
    15 oz), peeled and cut into 3 cm
    (1¼ inch) chunks
90 g (3¼ oz/½ cup) dried apricots
200 g (7 oz) green or yellow beans,
    trimmed
1½ teaspoons cornflour (cornstarch)

Preheat the oven to 160°C (315°F/Gas 2–3).

Tie the pork with string at 2 cm (¾ inch)
intervals to make a neat round shape. Lightly
brush with olive oil. Mix the cinnamon and cumin
together, then rub all over the pork.

Heat 1 tablespoon olive oil in a large
flameproof casserole dish or roasting tin. Add the
onion, celery and garlic and sauté for 5 minutes,
or until softened. Sit the pork in the dish, add
the thyme sprigs and pour in the cider. Bring to
a simmer, then cover and transfer to the oven.
Bake for 1½ hours, basting the pork occasionally.

Add the sweet potato and apricots, then cover
and cook for another 45 minutes. Add the beans,
cover again and cook for 15–20 minutes, or until
the sweet potato and beans are tender and the
pork is cooked through.

Remove the pork and vegetables to a large
dish or bowl and cover with foil to keep warm.

Place the casserole dish over high heat and
bring the liquid to the boil. Mix the cornflour with
1 tablespoon water to form a smooth paste, then
stir into the cooking liquid. Stirring constantly,
bring the mixture back to a simmer and cook
for 1–2 minutes, or until the sauce thickens.
Season well with sea salt and freshly ground
black pepper.

To serve, arrange the vegetables and apricots
on serving plates. Remove the string from the
pork, then cut the pork into slices 1 cm (½ inch)
thick and place two or three slices over the
vegetables. Spoon the juices over and serve.

Lamb chops with rosemary and almonds

4 lamb forequarter chops (about 1 kg/ 2 lb 4 oz)
1 tablespoon plain (all-purpose) flour
2 tablespoons olive oil
1 onion, cut into thin wedges
2 garlic cloves, chopped
4 celery stalks, cut into 4 cm (1½ inch) lengths
2 carrots, cut into thick batons
2 parsnips, peeled and cut into thick batons
1½ teaspoons ground cinnamon
1 teaspoon ground cumin
1 teaspoon ground sweet paprika
375 ml (13 fl oz/1½ cups) chicken or beef stock
1½ tablespoons honey
2 rosemary sprigs, plus extra, to serve
30 g (1 oz/¼ cup) toasted slivered almonds

Preheat the oven to 180°C (350°F/Gas 4).

Cut the chops in half lengthways down the centre, following their natural line and removing any excess fat. Pat the chops dry with paper towels, then dust with the flour, shaking off any excess.

Heat half the olive oil in a 3 litre (105 fl oz/ 12 cup) flameproof casserole dish. Add the chops in batches and cook over high heat for 3–4 minutes on each side, or until browned. Remove each batch to a plate.

Heat the remaining oil in the dish, then sauté the onion, garlic, celery, carrot and parsnip for 5–6 minutes, or until softened. Add the spices and cook, stirring, for 1 minute, or until fragrant.

Return the chops to the casserole, pushing them to the base of dish. Add the stock, honey and rosemary sprigs. Cover, then transfer to the oven and bake for 1 hour, or until the chops and vegetables are tender. Remove the rosemary sprigs and skim any fat from the surface of the casserole.

Arrange the chops and vegetables on serving plates. Spoon the sauce over, sprinkle with the almonds and some extra rosemary and serve.

* **Preparation time:** 20 minutes   * **Cooking time:** 1 hour 20 minutes   * **Serves:** 4

Preparation time: 15 minutes **Cooking time:** 3 hours 35 minutes **Serves:** 6

Roast beef with mustard, beer and parsnips

1.5 kg (3 lb 5 oz) beef bolar blade or
  corner-cut blade
2 tablespoons olive oil
6 pickling onions (about 350 g/12 oz
  in total), peeled
375 ml (13 fl oz/1½ cups) dark beer
750 ml (26 fl oz/3 cups) beef stock
2 tablespoons wholegrain mustard
2 bay leaves
4 thyme sprigs
2 parsnips, peeled and cut into 3 cm
  (1¼ inch) chunks
235 g (8½ oz/1½ cups) frozen peas
1 small handful flat-leaf (Italian) parsley,
  chopped

Preheat the oven to 150°C (300°F/Gas 2).

Season the beef well with sea salt and freshly ground black pepper. Heat the olive oil in a flameproof casserole dish over medium–high heat. Add the beef to the dish and cook, turning often, for 8–10 minutes, or until browned all over. Remove from the dish and set aside.

Reduce the heat to medium–low and sauté the onions for 5 minutes, or until golden. Return the beef to the dish, then add the beer, stock, mustard, bay leaves and thyme sprigs. Bring to the boil, reduce the heat to very low and cover tightly with foil or a lid. Transfer to the oven and bake for 1½ hours.

Add the parsnip and bake for a further 1–1½ hours, or until the beef and parsnip are very tender. Remove the beef and vegetables to a large plate, cover with foil and leave to rest while making the sauce.

Remove and discard the bay leaves and place the casserole dish on the stovetop over high heat. Bring the liquid to the boil, then reduce the heat to medium and simmer for 10 minutes. Add the peas and cook for another 10 minutes, or until the peas are tender and the liquid has reduced by half. Remove from the heat.

Return the beef and vegetables to the casserole to warm through. Remove the beef to a board and carve into thin slices. Divide among plates, then spoon the sauce and vegetables over. Scatter with the parsley and serve.

Mexican chicken bake

This recipe can also be made with minced (ground) beef instead of chicken thighs.

1 tablespoon peanut oil
4 chicken thigh fillets (about
   300 g/10½ oz), thinly sliced
2 spring onions (scallions), thinly sliced
1 teaspoon ground cumin
½ teaspoon chilli powder
420 g (15 oz) tin kidney beans, rinsed
   and drained
250 g (9 oz/2 cups) grated cheddar
   cheese
6 large flour tortillas
185 g (6½ oz/¾ cup) sour cream
1 large ripe avocado, chopped
40 g (1½ oz/⅓ cup) pitted black olives,
   sliced
shredded iceberg lettuce or baby cos
   (romaine) lettuce leaves, to serve

Tomato salsa sauce
1 small green capsicum (pepper),
   finely chopped
1 handful coriander (cilantro) leaves,
   chopped
2 garlic cloves, crushed
400 g (14 oz) tin chopped tomatoes
300 g (10½ oz/1 cup) chunky
   tomato salsa

Preheat the oven to 180°C (350°F/Gas 4).

For the tomato salsa sauce, put all the ingredients in a bowl, mix well and set aside.

Heat the oil in a large flameproof casserole dish over medium–high heat. Add the chicken, spring onion, cumin and chilli powder and sauté for 3–4 minutes, or until the chicken is lightly golden. Add the beans and tomato salsa sauce, stir together and remove from the heat.

Spread one-quarter of the chicken mixture in the casserole dish and sprinkle with 40 g (1½ oz/⅓ cup) of the cheese. Top with two of the tortillas, cutting where necessary to fit; the cheese layer should be covered. Repeat the layering with the remaining chicken mixture, cheese and tortillas, ending with a layer of cheese.

Cover with foil and bake for 15 minutes. Remove the foil and bake for 20–25 minutes more, or until the topping is golden and bubbling.

Divide among serving plates and top with a spoonful of sour cream and chopped avocado. Scatter with the olives and serve with lettuce.

Preparation time: 25 minutes   Cooking time: 45 minutes   Serves: 6

Fish baked in paper

600 g (1 lb 5 oz) fresh rice noodles

3 large bok choy (pak choy), leaves
trimmed, separated and cut in half

200 g (7 oz) snow peas (mangetout),
trimmed and thinly sliced lengthways

6 x 150 g (5½ oz) firm white fish fillets,
such as ling or monk fish

4 spring onions (scallions), trimmed
and thinly sliced on the diagonal

2 tablespoons very thinly sliced fresh
ginger

125 ml (4 fl oz/½ cup) soy sauce

125 ml (4 fl oz/½ cup) Chinese rice wine

Preheat the oven to 180ºC (350ºF/Gas 4).

Cut six sheets of baking paper about
30 cm (12 inches) square. Lay the sheets on
a work surface and divide the noodles among
them, placing the noodles in the middle of
each sheet and spreading them slightly to
form a single layer.

Divide the bok choy and snow peas among
the noodles, then place a fish fillet on each.
Sprinkle with the spring onion, ginger, soy sauce
and rice wine. Fold the short ends of the paper
in over the fish, then double-fold the long edges
together to seal and form tight parcels.

Place the parcels on a baking tray and bake
for 20–25 minutes, or until the fish is cooked
through and the vegetables are tender. Divide
the parcels among warm plates and serve.

Baking fish in paper is a good way
to retain all its juices; just be sure to
secure the parcel tightly all the way
around (small, pleat-like folds are
the most effective). Ordinary baking
paper is the best packaging, but if
you need to you can use doubled-up
sheets of foil, brushed well with oil
— take care not to tear holes in the
foil as it is not as robust as paper.

Sausages baked with potato and fennel

1 large handful flat-leaf (Italian) parsley
2 slices (65 g/2½ oz) day-old white bread
1 tablespoon olive oil
650 g (1 lb 7 oz) kipfler (fingerling) or
  other small potatoes, scrubbed and
  cut into 5 mm (¼ inch) slices
1 large fennel bulb, thinly sliced
3 garlic cloves, thinly sliced
400 g (14 oz) tin chopped tomatoes
1 bay leaf
1 teaspoon thyme leaves
80 ml (2½ fl oz/⅓ cup) white wine
185 ml (6 fl oz/¾ cup) chicken stock
  or water
6 thick Italian pork and fennel sausages
  (about 750 g/1 lb 10 oz in total)
green salad, to serve

Preheat the oven to 190°C (375°F/Gas 5).

Put the parsley and bread in a food processor and blend to make coarse crumbs. Add the olive oil and pulse to mix well. Spread the crumb mixture over the base of a 20 x 30 cm (8 x 12 inch) baking dish. Bake for 15–20 minutes, or until the crumbs are golden, then tip into a bowl, reserving the dish.

Place the potatoes, fennel, garlic, tomatoes, bay leaf and thyme in the baking dish. Toss to combine well, season well with sea salt and freshly ground black pepper, then spread the mixture evenly over the base of the dish. Pour the wine and stock over, then cover with foil and bake for 1 hour.

Add the sausages to the dish and bake, uncovered, for 45 minutes, or until the sausages are cooked through and the vegetables are very tender. Remove and discard the bay leaf, then scatter the reserved crumb mixture over and serve with a green salad.

Preparation time: 15 minutes   **Cooking time:** 2 hours   **Serves:** 6

Preparation time: 30 minutes
plus 1 hour proving

Cooking time: 30 minutes

Serves: 4

Deep-dish pizza

1½ teaspoons active dry yeast
½ teaspoon caster (superfine) sugar
335 g (11¾ oz/2¼ cups) plain
  (all-purpose) flour, approximately
1 teaspoon sea salt
2 tablespoons finely grated parmesan
  cheese
1 tablespoon olive oil

Topping
125 ml (4 fl oz/½ cup) tomato passata
  (puréed tomatoes)
a pinch of caster (superfine) sugar
265 g (9½ oz/1½ cups) shredded
  cooked chicken
1 small handful basil, some extra,
  to garnish
85 g (3 oz/⅓ cup) drained marinated
  roasted capsicum (pepper) strips
  (available from supermarkets)
2 bacon slices, cut into thin strips
200 g (7 oz) bocconcini (fresh baby
  mozzarella cheese), torn into chunks
olive oil, for drizzling (optional)

Combine the yeast, sugar and 250 ml (9 fl oz/ 1 cup) lukewarm water in a small bowl and leave in a warm place for 10 minutes, or until foamy.

Put the flour and salt in a large bowl, then stir in the parmesan, yeast mixture and olive oil. Turn out onto a lightly floured surface and knead for 5 minutes, or until the dough is smooth and elastic; if the dough is sticky you may need to add a little extra flour, but don't add too much or the dough will be tough. Place the dough in an oiled bowl, then cover and leave in a warm place for 1 hour, or until the dough has doubled in size.

Meanwhile, preheat the oven to 220°C (425°F/Gas 7). Lightly oil a round 28 cm (11¼ inch) baking tin that is at least 2.5 cm (1 inch) deep.

Turn the dough out onto a lightly floured surface and knead briefly until smooth. Roll the dough out until large enough to cover the base and side of the baking tin; the dough will be fairly thick. Press the sides of the dough into the tin to fit.

Mix together the passata and sugar and spread over the dough. Top with the chicken, basil, capsicum, bacon and bocconcini, then bake for 25–30 minutes, or until the dough is golden brown.

Sprinkle with extra basil, cut into wedges and serve immediately, drizzled with a little olive oil if desired.

Falso magro

Falso magro is a stuffed meat roll originally from Sicily.

To 'butterfly' the veal, cut it in half (but not completely through) along the length of the roast, leaving about 1.5 cm (⅝ inch) attached. Cut along the length through one side to the middle, leaving again about 1.5 cm (⅝ inch) attached; this forms a 'hinge' to open out the meat. Repeat on the other side. Open the meat out like a book, then flatten with a mallet.

1 kg (2 lb 4 oz) veal topside or veal rump roast, trimmed and butterflied (*see tip*, or ask your butcher to do this)
5 Italian pork sausages (500 g/1 lb 2 oz), casings removed
150 g (5½ oz) thinly sliced sopressa salami
1 large handful flat-leaf (Italian) parsley, chopped
65 g (2½ oz/¾ cup) grated pecorino cheese
4 bocconcini (fresh baby mozzarella cheese)
200 g (7 oz) thinly sliced prosciutto
100 g (3½ oz) provolone cheese, sliced and cut into pieces 1 cm (½ inch) wide
60 ml (2 fl oz/¼ cup) olive oil
125 ml (4 fl oz/½ cup) red wine
1 bay leaf
1 carrot, thinly sliced
1 celery stalk, thinly sliced
600 g (1 lb 5 oz) desiree or pontiac potatoes, peeled and cut into 3 cm (1¼ inch) chunks
250 ml (9 fl oz/1 cup) tomato passata (puréed tomatoes)
250 ml (9 fl oz/1 cup) chicken stock

Preheat the oven to 180°C (350°F/Gas 4).

Lay the veal out flat on a work surface and pound gently with a meat mallet to about 1.5 cm (⅝ inch) thick. Spread the sausage mince over the veal, leaving a 3 cm (1¼ inch) border around the edges. Lay the salami slices over the sausage; scatter the parsley over, then the grated pecorino. Wrap the bocconcini in the prosciutto, then lay them end to end across the middle length of the rectangle. Place the provolone pieces alongside. Fold over one side of the veal, then the other, to completely encase the filling. Tie securely with kitchen string at 2.5 cm (1 inch) intervals.

Heat the olive oil in a large, heavy-based flameproof roasting tin over medium–high heat. Add the veal roll, season with freshly ground black pepper and cook, turning often, for 10–12 minutes, or until browned all over.

Add the wine and cook for 2 minutes, or until it has reduced by half. Place the bay leaf, carrot, celery and potato around the meat. Combine the passata and stock, then pour around the meat. Cover the roasting tin with foil, sealing well. Transfer to the oven and bake for 1 hour, basting with the passata mixture every 20 minutes. Remove from the oven and allow the veal to rest for 20 minutes before carving.

Cut the veal roll into 2 cm (¾ inch) slices. Serve with the vegetables, with the cooking liquid spooned over.

Preparation time: 30 minutes
plus 20 minutes resting

Cooking time: 1 hour 15 minutes

Serves: 8

Preparation time: 25 minutes   **Cooking time:** 3 hours   **Serves:** 6

Beef bourguignon with garlic toasts

60 g (2¼ oz) unsalted butter

1.5 kg (3 lb 5 oz) gravy beef or oyster blade, cut into 3 cm (1¼ inch) chunks

150 g (5½ oz) button mushrooms, trimmed and wiped clean

2 tablespoons olive oil

200 g (7 oz) smoked pork or smoked rindless bacon, cut into 2 cm (¾ inch) pieces

12 small pickling onions (about 400 g/ 14 oz in total), peeled

1 onion, finely chopped

2 garlic cloves, finely chopped

1½ tablespoons plain (all-purpose) flour

435 ml (15¼ fl oz/1¾ cups) red wine

310 ml (10¾ fl oz/1¼ cups) beef stock

1 tablespoon tomato paste (concentrated purée)

1 bouquet garni, made with 1 bay leaf, 3 sprigs thyme and 3 sprigs parsley

100 g (3½ oz) English spinach leaves, roughly chopped

2 tablespoons chopped flat-leaf (Italian) parsley

Garlic toasts

30 g (1 oz) butter, softened

2 garlic cloves, crushed

1 small baguette, cut into 6 slices, each 1 cm (½ inch) thick

Preheat the oven to 175°C (335°F/Gas 3–4).

Melt half the butter in a large flameproof casserole dish over medium heat. Add the beef in batches and cook, turning often, for 5 minutes, or until well browned, removing each batch to a plate.

Add the mushrooms to the dish and sauté for 1 minute, then remove the mushrooms to a bowl. Add the remaining butter and the olive oil to the dish and sauté the pork, pickling onions, chopped onion and garlic for 8 minutes, or until the onions are well browned.

Return the beef to the casserole. Stir in the flour to coat the mixture and cook for 2 minutes. Stir in the wine, then add the stock, tomato paste and bouquet garni. Season with sea salt and freshly ground black pepper. Bring to the boil, then cover, transfer to the oven and bake for 2 hours.

For the garlic toasts, mix together the butter and garlic and spread over one side of each baguette slice. Remove the bouquet garni from the casserole and discard, then stir in the reserved mushrooms and the spinach. Arrange the baguette slices over the top, buttered side up. Bake, uncovered, for a further 30 minutes, or until the topping is golden and the beef is very tender.

Scatter with the parsley and serve.

If the casserole appears to be drying out during cooking, press a sheet of baking paper over the surface and replace the lid. Remove the paper and lid when adding the baguette layer.

Swedish spinach meatballs

3 slices white bread (about 90 g/3¼ oz),
  crusts removed
125 ml (4 fl oz/½ cup) milk
1 red onion, very finely chopped
500 g (1 lb 2 oz) minced (ground) pork
2 egg yolks
1 teaspoon hot English mustard
½ teaspoon freshly grated nutmeg
250 g (9 oz) packet frozen spinach,
  thawed and squeezed dry
2 tablespoons light olive oil
20 g (¾ oz) butter
35 g (1¼ oz/¼ cup) plain (all-purpose)
  flour
375 ml (13 fl oz/1½ cups) beef stock
450 g (1 lb) red potatoes, peeled and
  roughly grated
185 ml (6 fl oz/¾ cup) cream
dill sprigs, to garnish
lingonberry preserve or cranberry sauce,
  to serve

Preheat the oven to 200°C (400°F/Gas 6).

Place the bread and milk in a small bowl and leave to soak for 2 minutes.

Put the onion, pork, egg yolks, mustard, nutmeg and spinach in a bowl. Squeeze out the excess milk from the bread, then add the bread to the pork mixture. Season well with sea salt and freshly ground black pepper, then mix the ingredients together using clean hands. Roll into 12 evenly sized balls.

Heat half the olive oil and half the butter in a flameproof casserole dish or baking dish over medium heat. Add the meatballs, in batches if necessary, and cook for 5 minutes, or until golden brown, turning often. Remove the meatballs to a plate.

Add the flour to the dish with the remaining oil and butter, stirring constantly. Slowly pour in the stock, stirring to make a smooth sauce. Return the meatballs to the dish. Cover the meatballs with the grated potato, then drizzle the cream over.

Transfer to the oven and bake for 35 minutes, or until the potato topping is golden and crisp. Garnish with dill sprigs and serve with lingonberry preserve or cranberry sauce.

Preparation time: 30 minutes   Cooking time: 45 minutes   Serves: 4–6

Preparation time: 25 minutes   **Cooking time:** 1 hour 15 minutes   **Serves:** 6

Baked fish with potato and fennel gratin

50 g (1¾ oz) butter
4 potatoes (about 800 g/1 lb 12 oz)
2 small fennel bulbs
2 bacon slices, finely chopped
130 g (4½ oz/1 cup) grated gruyère
   cheese
185 ml (6 fl oz/¾ cup) cream
2 tablespoons thinly snipped chives
6 x 175 g (6 oz) firm white fish fillets
   (such as snapper, barramundi, ling,
   ocean perch)
lemon wedges, to serve

Preheat the oven to 180°C (350°F/Gas 4).
Grease a 19 x 28 cm (7½ x 11¼ inch)
rectangular ceramic baking dish with
1 tablespoon of the butter.

Peel and finely slice the potatoes, place
in a bowl and cover with water to stop them
discolouring. Trim and finely slice the fennel
bulbs, then place in another bowl and cover with
water. Drain the potatoes and fennel well. Overlap
half the potato slices in the baking dish to form
a layer. Top with half the fennel slices, then
sprinkle with half the bacon and half the gruyère.
Repeat with the remaining potato, fennel, bacon
and gruyère, finishing with a layer of gruyère.

Whisk the cream with half the chives, then
pour over the potato mixture. Lightly grease a
sheet of foil with some of the butter and cover
the dish firmly with the foil. Bake for 45 minutes,
then remove and reserve the foil and bake for a
further 15 minutes, or until the potato is tender
and the cheese is golden.

Mix the remaining chives and butter in a
small bowl. Season the fish fillets with sea salt
and freshly ground black pepper, then spread the
butter mixture evenly over the fish. Return the
sheet of foil to the baking dish and place the fish
over the top.

Bake for a further 12–15 minutes, or until
the fish is just cooked through. Divide the fish
among serving plates. Slice the gratin, arrange
on the plates and drizzle with the cooking juices.
Serve immediately, with lemon wedges.

Lamb bobotie

2 tablespoons butter
1 large onion, finely chopped
2 garlic cloves, crushed
1 teaspoon grated fresh ginger
1 granny smith apple, peeled and
  chopped
2 tablespoons mild Indian-style
  curry powder
1 teaspoon ground cumin
600 g (1 lb 5 oz) minced (ground) lamb
2 slices of white bread, soaked in
  60 ml (2 fl oz/¼ cup) milk
1 tablespoon soft brown sugar
60 g (2¼ oz/½ cup) raisins
2 tablespoons slivered almonds
2 tablespoons lemon juice
3 eggs
250 ml (9 fl oz/1 cup) milk
1 bay leaf
mango chutney, to serve
green salad, to serve

Preheat the oven to 180°C (350°F/Gas 4).

Melt the butter in a 3 litre (105 fl oz/12 cup) flameproof casserole dish over medium heat. Add the onion, garlic and ginger and sauté for 5 minutes, or until the onion has softened. Add the apple, curry powder and cumin and sauté for another 3 minutes, or until fragrant. Remove from the heat and leave to cool slightly.

Put the lamb and soaked bread in a bowl and mix well, using your hands. Add the sugar, raisins, almonds, lemon juice and two of the eggs. Add the onion mixture, reserving the casserole dish. Season with sea salt and freshly ground black pepper and mix together well.

Spoon the lamb mixture into the casserole dish, pressing down firmly and smoothing the surface even. Bake for 30 minutes, or until cooked through.

Beat the milk and the remaining egg in a small bowl until well combined. Remove the casserole from the oven and use the fork to create small holes on the surface of the lamb mixture. Pour the milk mixture over and place the bay leaf on top. Bake for a further 20–25 minutes, or until the topping has set and is golden.

Slice the hot bobotie, or spoon onto plates. Serve with mango chutney and a green salad.

Preparation time: 15 minutes   Cooking time: 1 hour   Serves: 4

Preparation time: 30 minutes   **Cooking time:** 45 minutes   **Serves:** 4–6

Bread bake with salami, spinach and gruyère

8 eggs, lightly beaten

1 teaspoon mustard powder

1 litre (35 fl oz/4 cups) milk

300 g (10½ oz) day-old baguette,
cut into slices 5 mm (¼ inch) thick

100 g (3½ oz) salami, thinly sliced and
cut into 1 cm (½ inch) strips

70 g (2½ oz/½ cup) chopped semi-dried
(sun-blushed) tomatoes

1 large handful baby English spinach
leaves

130 g (4½ oz/1 cup) grated gruyère
cheese

3 tablespoons torn basil leaves

2 tablespoons snipped chives

1 tablespoon chopped flat-leaf (Italian)
parsley, plus extra, to serve

Preheat the oven to 190°C (375°F/Gas 5).
Grease a 2 litre (70 fl oz/8 cup) rectangular
baking dish.

In a large bowl, whisk together the eggs,
mustard and milk until well combined. Season
with sea salt and freshly ground black pepper
and set aside.

Place a layer of bread, overlapping the slices
slightly, over the base of the baking dish, then
scatter with some of the salami strips, tomatoes,
spinach, cheese and herbs. Continue layering
until all the ingredients are used, finishing with
a layer of bread. Pour the milk mixture over the
bread, then allow to stand for 10 minutes, so
that the liquid can be absorbed.

Cover with foil and bake for 25 minutes.
Remove the foil, then bake for another
20 minutes, or until the surface is crisp and
golden brown and the bake is firm in the middle.
Remove from the oven and allow to cool slightly.
Scatter with extra parsley and serve.

For a different flavour, replace the
salami with slices of smoked ham
cut off the bone, and instead of the
basil use a tablespoon of chopped
sage leaves.

Lamb and broad bean hotpot with polenta dumplings

1 tablespoon olive oil

1 onion, chopped

1 celery stalk, chopped

1 small red capsicum (pepper), diced

2 garlic cloves, chopped

1 tablespoon plain (all-purpose) flour

1 kg (2 lb 4 oz) boneless lamb shoulder, trimmed and cut into 3 cm (1¼ inch) chunks

1 teaspoon dried oregano

1 orange sweet potato (about 300 g/ 10½ oz), peeled and cut into 4 cm (1½ inch) chunks

175 g (6 oz/1 cup) fresh or thawed frozen broad (fava) beans

500 ml (17 fl oz/2 cups) tomato passata (puréed tomatoes)

150 g (5½ oz/1 cup) instant polenta

60 ml (2 fl oz/¼ cup) cream

50 g (¾ oz/½ cup) grated parmesan cheese

1 tablespoon chopped parsley, plus extra, to serve

Preheat the oven to 150°C (300°F/Gas 2). Heat the olive oil in a large flameproof casserole dish. Add the onion, celery, capsicum and garlic and sauté over medium heat for 5 minutes, or until softened slightly.

Sprinkle the flour over, stir to combine well, then gradually add 185 ml (6 fl oz/¾ cup) water, mixing until smooth. Add the lamb, oregano, sweet potato, broad beans and passata. Bring to a simmer and season well with sea salt and freshly ground black pepper. Cover, then transfer to the oven and bake for 2 hours, stirring occasionally, until the lamb is tender and the sauce is reduced and thick. Increase the oven temperature to 180°C (350°F/Gas 4).

Meanwhile, put the polenta in a heatproof bowl and pour 310 ml (10¾ fl oz/1¼ cups) boiling water over, whisking to combine well. Leave to stand for 3–4 minutes, or until thick. Season well, then stir in the cream, half the parmesan and all the parsley.

Spoon the polenta mixture in big dollops over the meat mixture and sprinkle with the remaining parmesan. Bake, uncovered, for 20 minutes, or until the dumplings are cooked through and lightly golden. Remove from the oven and leave to stand for 15 minutes to cool slightly. Sprinkle with parsley before serving.

Preparation time: 20 minutes **Cooking time:** 2 hours 30 minutes **Serves:** 4–6

Preparation time: 25 minutes   **Cooking time:** 1 hour   **Serves:** 4–6

Vegetable biryani with cumin pastry

2 tablespoons vegetable oil

2 onions, thinly sliced

2 garlic cloves, crushed

1 tablespoon finely chopped fresh ginger

1 green chilli, seeded and finely chopped

2 teaspoons garam masala

1 tablespoon curry powder

125 g (4½ oz/½ cup) Greek-style yoghurt,
  plus extra, to serve

60 ml (2 fl oz/¼ cup) lime juice

400 g (14 oz) pumpkin (winter squash),
  peeled and cut into 4 cm (1½ inch)
  chunks

2 potatoes, peeled and cut into 2 cm
  (¾ inch) chunks

½ cauliflower, cut into small florets
  (about 420 g/15 oz/3½ cups)

2 carrots, cut into 2 cm (¾ inch) chunks

200 g (7 oz/1 cup) basmati rice

175 g (6 oz) green beans, trimmed and
  cut into 4 cm (1½ inch) lengths

2 tomatoes, cut into 2 cm (¾ inch) dice

750 ml (26 fl oz/3 cups) vegetable stock

a pinch of saffron threads

40 g (1½ oz/⅓ cup) sultanas (golden
  raisins)

1 sheet frozen shortcrust pastry, thawed

1 egg, lightly beaten

1 teaspoon cumin seeds

coriander (cilantro) leaves, to garnish

2 tablespoons toasted cashew nuts,
  roughly chopped

Preheat the oven to 180°C (350°F/Gas 4).

Heat the oil in a 3 litre (105 fl oz/12 cup) flameproof casserole dish over medium–high heat. Add the onion and garlic and sauté for 5 minutes, or until golden. Add the ginger, chilli and spices and cook for a further 2 minutes, or until aromatic. Stir in the yoghurt and lime juice, then add the pumpkin, potato, cauliflower and carrot.

Stir the rice through, then add the beans, tomato, stock, saffron and sultanas. Mix well and bring to the boil.

Remove the dish from the heat, then carefully cover the top with the pastry, trimming if necessary and sealing the pastry well to ensure no steam escapes. Brush the top with beaten egg and sprinkle with the cumin seeds.

Bake for 40 minutes, or until the pastry is golden. Remove from the oven and leave to stand for 5 minutes. Divide into serving portions and transfer to warm plates. Serve garnished with coriander, with extra yoghurt for drizzling and with chopped cashews for sprinkling over.

Chicken with pine nut, caper and currant stuffing

If ready-made aïoli is not available, stir a crushed garlic clove through some whole-egg mayonnaise instead.

6 chicken thigh fillets (about 800 g/
  1 lb 12 oz), skin left on
12 thin slices of centre-cut bacon
2 tablespoons extra virgin olive oil
375 ml (13 fl oz/1½ cups) red wine
375 ml (13 fl oz/1½ cups) chicken stock
1 tablespoon balsamic vinegar
2½ teaspoons caster (superfine) sugar
500 g (1 lb 2 oz) baby potatoes, halved
300 g (10½ oz) broccolini, cut lengthways
  into long, thin florets
ready-made aïoli, to serve (optional)

Pine nut, caper and currant stuffing
100 g (3½ oz/1¼ cups) fresh
  breadcrumbs
55 g (2 oz/¼ cup) chopped pitted
  green olives
3 anchovy fillets, finely chopped
2½ tablespoons baby capers, rinsed
  and drained
40 g (1½ oz/¼ cup) pine nuts, chopped
1 small garlic clove, finely chopped
35 g (1¼ oz/¼ cup) currants
2½ tablespoons chopped flat-leaf (Italian)
  parsley
65 g (2½ oz/¾ cup) grated pecorino
  cheese
1 egg, lightly beaten

Preheat the oven to 180°C (350°F/Gas 4).

Place one chicken thigh, skin side down, on a board. Using a sharp knife and holding it at a 45-degree angle to the chicken, make cuts in the meat to butterfly it open, taking care not to cut all the way through the chicken. Use a meat mallet to carefully pound each thigh out to measure roughly 16 x 18 cm (6¼ x 7 inches). Repeat with the remaining chicken thighs.

Put the stuffing ingredients in a bowl, season with sea salt and freshly ground black pepper and mix well. Working one at a time, divide the stuffing among the chicken pieces, pressing it on firmly; carefully roll each one up. Slightly overlap two bacon slices on a board, then place a rolled chicken thigh on the bacon slices and carefully roll the bacon around to enclose. Using kitchen string, tie the bacon at 2 cm (¾ inch) intervals to hold it in place. Repeat to form six neat bundles.

Heat the olive oil in a large flameproof casserole dish. Cook the chicken rolls over medium heat, turning often, for 5 minutes, or until browned all over. Add the wine, stock, vinegar, sugar and potatoes. Bring to a simmer, then reduce the heat to low; cover and simmer for 15 minutes. Place the broccolini over the chicken, then cover and simmer for another 15 minutes, or until the vegetables are tender and the chicken is cooked through.

Remove the vegetables and chicken to a bowl and cover to keep warm. Increase the heat to high and boil the cooking liquid for 10–15 minutes, or until reduced by half. Untie the chicken rolls, then return them to the pan with the vegetables to warm through. Remove the chicken parcels, cut each in half on the diagonal and divide among warm shallow bowls with the vegetables. Spoon the sauce over and serve, with aïoli if desired.

Preparation time: 40 minutes   Cooking time: 55 minutes   Serves: 6

✳ **Preparation time:** 25 minutes   ✳ **Cooking time:** 1 hour 45 minutes   ✳ **Serves:** 4–6

Roast pork with apples, pumpkin and chestnut gravy

1.5 kg (3 lb 5 oz) boneless leg of pork, rolled, tied with string and skin scored (ask your butcher to do this)

2 large thyme sprigs, cut into 1 cm (½ inch) lengths

3 garlic cloves, cut into thin slivers

1 tablespoon olive oil

6 small red apples, such as pink lady (about 750 g/1 lb 10 oz)

600 g (1 lb 5 oz) pumpkin (winter squash), cut into 5 cm (2 inch) wedges

60 ml (2 fl oz/¼ cup) dry sherry

250 ml (9 fl oz/1 cup) chicken stock

100 g (3½ oz/1 cup) whole chestnuts, either tinned and drained, or frozen and thawed

watercress sprigs, to serve

Preheat the oven to 240°C (475°F/Gas 8).

Using a small sharp knife, cut slits in the pork flesh (but not in the skin), then push the thyme sprigs and garlic into the slits. Brush the pork all over with the olive oil and season well with sea salt and freshly ground black pepper; rub the salt generously into the pork skin to help the crackling form. Place the pork in a large flameproof roasting tin and roast for 35 minutes, or until the skin is golden and crisp.

Reduce the oven temperature to 180°C (350°F/Gas 4). Add the apples and pumpkin to the roasting tin and roast for 1 hour, or until the apples and pumpkin are tender and the juices run clear when a skewer is inserted into the centre of the pork.

Transfer the pork, apples and pumpkin to a large plate and cover loosely with foil; keep warm. Spoon off as much fat as you can from the juices in the roasting tin. Place the roasting tin over medium heat, then stir in the sherry and stock, scraping the base of the tin to remove any cooked-on pieces of meat. Simmer for 1–2 minutes, then add the chestnuts and simmer for another 5 minutes, or until the juices are reduced by half and the chestnuts are warmed through. Set aside to keep warm.

Carve the pork into slices 1 cm (½ inch) thick. Serve the pork, apples and pumpkin with the chestnuts and the gravy spooned over, scattered with watercress sprigs.

Turkey polpettoni with capsicum and olive sauce

You can replace the turkey in this recipe with minced (ground) chicken, veal or beef.

2 tablespoons olive oil
2 red capsicums (peppers), cut lengthways into 1 cm (½ inch) strips
125 ml (4 fl oz/½ cup) white wine
685 ml (23½ fl oz/2¾ cups) tomato passata (puréed tomatoes)
155 g (5½ oz/1¼ cups) black pitted olives
rocket (arugula), to serve
grated parmesan cheese, to serve

Turkey meatballs
2 slices white bread, cut into 1 cm (½ inch) pieces
60 ml (2 fl oz/¼ cup) milk
1 kg (2 lb 4 oz) minced (ground) turkey
3 garlic cloves, finely chopped
100 g (3½ oz) prosciutto, finely chopped
200 g (7 oz) Italian pork and fennel sausages, casings removed
1 egg
25 g (1 oz/¼ cup) grated parmesan cheese
1 small handful flat-leaf (Italian) parsley, finely chopped
¼ teaspoon ground nutmeg

For the turkey meatballs, put all the ingredients in a large bowl. Season with sea salt and freshly ground black pepper and mix together well using your hands. With damp hands, shape the mixture into 3 cm (1¼ inch) balls and place on a tray. Cover and refrigerate for 1 hour.

Meanwhile, preheat the oven to 220°C (425°F/Gas 7).

Pour the olive oil into a large baking dish and place in the oven to heat for 5 minutes.

Add the meatballs to the baking dish and bake for 10 minutes, turning occasionally, until brown all over. Add the capsicum strips and cook for 10 minutes, or until softened.

Reduce the oven temperature to 180°C (350°F/Gas 4). Add the wine, passata and olives to the dish and bake for 20–30 minutes, or until the sauce has thickened slightly and the meatballs are cooked through. Serve with rocket and sprinkle with parmesan.

Preparation time: 40 minutes
plus 1 hour chilling

Cooking time: 1 hour

Serves: 6

Baked Spanish omelette

a large pinch of saffron threads
  (optional)
60 ml (2 fl oz/¼ cup) olive oil
1 desiree potato, peeled and cut
  into 1 cm (½ inch) chunks
1 onion, finely chopped
2 garlic cloves, crushed
115 g (4 oz/¾ cup) chopped leg ham
185 g (6½ oz/1 cup) peeled broad
  (fava) beans
6 large eggs, lightly beaten
1 small handful flat-leaf (Italian) parsley,
  finely chopped

If using the saffron, put it in a small cup
with 1 tablespoon hot water. Stand at room
temperature for 1 hour to infuse.

Preheat the oven to 200°C (400°F/Gas 6).

In an ovenproof frying pan with an 18 cm
(7 inch) base, heat the olive oil. Add the potato
and cook over medium heat for 8–10 minutes,
or until just tender, turning occasionally.

Add the onion and garlic to the pan and sauté
over medium–low heat for 5 minutes, or until
the onion has softened. Add the ham and broad
beans and cook for 2–3 minutes, then press the
vegetables down in the pan with the back of a
wooden spoon until the surface is even.

Combine the eggs and parsley in a small bowl
with the saffron mixture, if using; mix well. Pour
over the potato mixture and season with sea salt
and freshly ground pepper. Transfer the pan to
the oven and bake the omelette for 10 minutes,
or until golden and set in the middle.

Invert the omelette onto a plate. Cut into
wedges and serve warm.

This is a great way to use up
left-over baked vegetables such
as pumpkin (winter squash), potato,
carrot, parsnip and fennel. Use any
combination you like; simply add
them to the base mixture before
adding the eggs.

Baked chicken, pea and prosciutto risotto

You can easily vary the flavours here — for example, use leeks instead of the peas, and bacon or pancetta instead of prosciutto (add these with the rice). Drained tinned chickpeas, white beans or borlotti beans would also work well in place of the peas, and if you don't have chicken breasts, chicken thigh fillets are very suitable. For added richness, you could even stir in a little blue or mascarpone cheese at the end.

2 tablespoons olive oil
20 g (¾ oz) butter
1 large onion, finely chopped
2 garlic cloves, crushed
2 teaspoons thyme leaves, chopped
275 g (9¾ oz/1¼ cups) arborio rice
1.5 litres (52 fl oz/6 cups) chicken stock
2 x 150 g (5½ oz) skinless chicken breast fillets, cut into 5 mm (¼ inch) slices
155 g (5½ oz/1 cup) frozen peas, thawed
100 g (3½ oz) prosciutto, torn into 3 cm (1¼ inch) strips
25 g (1 oz/¼ cup) finely grated parmesan cheese
1 small handful flat-leaf (Italian) parsley, chopped

Preheat the oven to 180°C (350°F/Gas 4).

Heat the olive oil and butter in a large flameproof casserole dish over medium heat until the butter has melted. Add the onion and garlic and sauté for 5 minutes, or until the onion is lightly golden.

Add the thyme and rice and cook, stirring, for 1 minute, or until the rice is coated with the butter mixture. Pour in the stock, then bring to the boil over high heat, stirring continuously. Cover, transfer to the oven and bake for 15 minutes.

Stir in the chicken and peas, then cover and bake for another 15 minutes, or until the chicken is cooked through and the rice and peas are tender. Gently stir in the prosciutto, parmesan and parsley and serve immediately.

Preparation time: 30 minutes ✳ **Cooking time:** 40 minutes ✳ **Serves:** 4

Capsicums stuffed with lamb and couscous

6 x 150–180 g (5½–6 oz) red or yellow
  capsicums (peppers)
140 g (5 oz/¾ cup) instant couscous
2½ tablespoons olive oil
1 onion, grated
2 garlic cloves, chopped
1 teaspoon ground cumin
2 teaspoons ground coriander
½ teaspoon ground allspice
a large pinch of chilli flakes (optional)
1 small handful chopped flat-leaf
  (Italian) parsley
1 small handful chopped mint
1 teaspoon finely grated lemon rind
250 g (9 oz) minced (ground) lamb
65 g (2½ oz/½ cup) chopped pistachio
  nuts
500 ml (17 fl oz/2 cups) tomato passata
  (puréed tomatoes)

Preheat the oven to 190°C (375°F/Gas 5).

Cut the tops off the capsicums and reserve. Discard the membranes and seeds from inside the capsicums.

Place the couscous in a large heatproof bowl. Pour 125 ml (4 fl oz/½ cup) boiling water over, then cover and leave to stand for 3–5 minutes, or until the water is absorbed. Stir in 1 tablespoon of the olive oil, using a fork to break up any lumps. Stir in the onion, garlic, spices, herbs and lemon rind. Add the lamb and pistachios, then season well with sea salt and freshly ground black pepper. Mix thoroughly, using your hands.

Spoon the mixture into the capsicum cavities. Stand the capsicums in a baking dish in which they will all fit snugly. Place the reserved capsicum lids on top.

Combine the passata with 250 ml (9 fl oz/ 1 cup) water and pour into the baking dish, around the capsicums. Drizzle the remaining oil over the capsicums. Cover with foil and bake for 20 minutes, then remove the foil and bake for another 25 minutes, or until the filling is cooked and the capsicums are tender.

Serve hot or at room temperature, with the passata sauce.

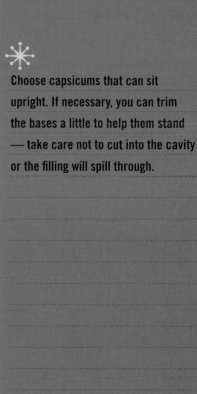

Choose capsicums that can sit upright. If necessary, you can trim the bases a little to help them stand — take care not to cut into the cavity or the filling will spill through.

Simple cassoulet

80 ml (2½ fl oz/⅓ cup) olive oil
4 thin merguez sausages, or other
    fresh thin sausages
4 chicken thigh fillets, cut into
    slices 2 cm (¾ inch) thick
1 small onion, halved and thinly sliced
3 garlic cloves, sliced
½ teaspoon fennel seeds
150 g (5½ oz) piece of smoked bacon,
    cut into 2 cm (¾ inch) chunks
80 ml (2½ fl oz/⅓ cup) white wine
500 ml (17 fl oz/2 cups) chicken stock
1 bay leaf
2 x 400 g (14 oz) tins white beans (such
    as haricot, cannellini or butterbeans/
    lima beans), rinsed and drained
8 baby carrots, trimmed
400 g (14 oz) tin chopped tomatoes
1 tablespoon tomato paste (concentrated
    purée)
1 tablespoon chopped flat-leaf (Italian)
    parsley
160 g (5½ oz/2 cups) fresh breadcrumbs

Heat half the olive oil in a flameproof casserole dish over medium heat. Add the sausages and chicken and cook, turning often, for 5 minutes, or until browned all over. Remove to a plate and set aside.

Add the onion, garlic, fennel seeds and bacon to the dish and sauté for 5–8 minutes, or until the onion has softened. Return the sausages and chicken to the dish, then pour in the wine and cook until only a tablespoon of the liquid remains.

Add the stock, bay leaf, beans, carrots, tomatoes and tomato paste, then pour in enough water to just cover the ingredients. Bring to the boil, then reduce the heat to low and simmer for 40 minutes, or until most of the liquid has been absorbed. Season to taste with sea salt and freshly ground black pepper and stir in the parsley.

Meanwhile, preheat the oven to 190°C (375°F/Gas 5).

Combine the breadcrumbs and remaining oil in a bowl, tossing to coat the crumbs. Scatter them evenly over the cassoulet and bake for 30–40 minutes, or until the crumbs are golden.

Preparation time: 15 minutes **Cooking time:** 1 hour 40 minutes **Serves:** 4

* **Preparation time:** 30 minutes   * **Cooking time:** 50 minutes   * **Serves:** 4

Tomato, bacon and egg lasagne

250 g (9 oz/1 cup) ricotta cheese

125 ml (4 fl oz/½ cup) cream

½ teaspoon freshly grated nutmeg

50 g (1¾ oz/½ cup) grated parmesan cheese

125 g (4½ oz/1 cup) grated cheddar cheese

1 tablespoon olive oil

1 onion, chopped

3 bacon slices, cut into 1 cm (½ inch) pieces

500 ml (17 fl oz/2 cups) tomato pasta sauce

2–3 large fresh lasagne sheets

4 eggs

250 g (9 oz) packet frozen chopped spinach, thawed and squeezed dry

flat-leaf (Italian) parsley leaves, to garnish

Preheat the oven to 180°C (350°F/Gas 4).

Put the ricotta, cream, nutmeg, parmesan and half the cheddar in a bowl. Mix well and set aside.

Heat the olive oil in a large wide (4 litre/ 140 fl oz/16 cup) flameproof casserole dish. Sauté the onion and bacon over medium heat for 5–7 minutes, or until the bacon is cooked. Remove to a plate and take the dish off the heat.

Spread one-third of the tomato sauce over the base of the dish, then cover with a lasagne sheet, cutting the lasagne to fit. Spread half the onion mixture over and another one-third of the sauce.

Make four small, evenly spaced wells in the sauce and break the eggs into them. Cover with another layer of lasagne sheets.

Spread the remaining onion mixture over, then dot with the spinach and half the ricotta mixture. Top with a third layer of lasagne sheets. Pour the remaining ricotta mixture over, spoon the remaining tomato sauce over and sprinkle with the remaining cheddar.

Bake for 40 minutes, or until the lasagne sheets are cooked and the topping is golden. Remove from the oven and leave to stand for 10 minutes. Sprinkle with parsley leaves before serving.

You will only need two or three lasagne sheets from the packet. Seal the pack and freeze the remaining sheets for later use — you just need to thaw them before using them in another recipe.

Baked tuna and cauliflower frittata

2 tablespoons olive oil
½ cauliflower (about 600 g/1 lb 5 oz), trimmed and cut into small florets
2 garlic cloves, crushed
3 anchovy fillets, finely chopped
8 eggs
185 ml (6 fl oz/¾ cup) cream
2 tablespoons finely chopped chervil, plus extra sprigs, to garnish
50 g (1¾ oz/½ cup) finely grated parmesan cheese
2 tablespoons chopped raisins
425 g (15 oz) tin tuna in oil, drained and flaked with a fork
balsamic vinegar, for drizzling
extra virgin olive oil, for drizzling
chervil sprigs, to garnish
green salad, to serve
crusty bread, to serve

Preheat the oven to 165°C (320°F/Gas 3).

Heat 1½ tablespoons of the olive oil in a 24 cm (9½ inch) ovenproof non-stick frying pan. Add the cauliflower, garlic and anchovy and toss to coat the cauliflower. Cover the pan with foil, transfer to the oven and bake for 15–20 minutes, or until the caulilflower is tender.

Meanwhile, break the eggs into a large bowl and lightly beat. Add the cream, chervil and half the parmesan and whisk to combine well. Stir in the raisins and tuna and season with sea salt and freshly ground black pepper.

Add the baked cauliflower mixture to the egg mixture and mix together well.

Wipe the hot frying pan clean, then add the remaining oil, swirling the pan to coat the base. Pour in the egg mixture, sprinkle with the remaining parmesan and bake for 35 minutes, or until golden and firm to the touch.

Remove the frittata from the oven and allow to stand for 10 minutes, then cut into wedges and divide among serving plates. Drizzle with vinegar and olive oil and sprinkle with chervil. Serve with a green salad and crusty bread.

Preparation time: 15 minutes   **Cooking time:** 55 minutes   **Serves:** 6

Preparation time: 30 minutes
plus overnight soaking

Cooking time: 2 hours

Serves: 4–6

Ham baked beans with cheesy cornbread crust

300 g (10½ oz/1½ cups) dried red
   kidney beans
1 smoked ham hock (about 600 g/
   1 lb 5 oz), skin removed
1 tablespoon olive oil
1 onion, finely chopped
2 garlic cloves, finely chopped
1 green chilli, seeded and chopped
425 g tin (15 oz) tomato passata
   (puréed tomatoes)
1 tablespoon treacle, golden syrup or
   light or dark corn syrup
2 tablespoons worcestershire sauce
2 tablespoons barbecue sauce
1 tablespoon dijon mustard
½ teaspoon freshly ground black pepper

Cornbread crust

150 g (5½ oz/1 cup) plain (all-purpose)
   flour
3½ teaspoons baking powder
150 g (5½ oz/1 cup) polenta
½ teaspoon sea salt
1 tablespoon soft brown sugar
250 ml (9 fl oz/1 cup) milk
60 ml (2 fl oz/¼ cup) olive oil
1 egg, lightly beaten
125 g (4½ oz/1 cup) grated cheddar
   cheese
125 g (4½ oz) tin corn kernels,
   drained well

Place the beans in a large bowl, pour in enough cold water to cover well, then leave to soak overnight.

Preheat the oven to 200°C (400°F/Gas 6).

Drain the beans well and place in a large flameproof casserole dish with the ham hock. Pour in enough cold water to cover, then bring to the boil over medium heat. Reduce the heat to low and simmer for 50–60 minutes, or until the beans are tender. Remove the ham hock and set aside. Drain the beans, reserving 375 ml (13 fl oz/1½ cups) of the cooking liquid, and set aside.

Remove the meat from the ham hock, discard the bones and excess fat, then shred the meat using a fork. Set aside.

Wipe the casserole dish dry, then place over medium heat with the olive oil. Add the onion, garlic and chilli and sauté for 2 minutes, then add the reserved cooking liquid, passata, treacle, worcestershire sauce, barbecue sauce, mustard, black pepper, the beans and the meat from the ham hock. Simmer over low heat for 30 minutes, or until the beans are soft and tender and the liquid has thickened.

To make the cornbread crust, sift the flour and baking powder into a large bowl. Stir in the polenta, sea salt and sugar, then make a well in the centre. Add the milk, olive oil, egg, cheese and corn and mix together to make a dough.

Spoon the dough evenly over the beans. Bake for 20–25 minutes, or until the crust is cooked through and golden brown. Serve hot.

Roast chicken with brussels sprouts, bacon and chestnuts

2 kg (4 lb 8 oz) whole free-range chicken
1 lemon, halved
6 thyme sprigs
25 g (1 oz) butter, softened
500 g (1 lb 2 oz) baby potatoes
400 g (14 oz) brussels sprouts, trimmed
  and tough outer leaves removed
300 g (10½ oz) frozen peeled chestnuts,
  thawed (*see tip*)
2 bacon slices, cut crossways into
  2.5 cm (1 inch) pieces
2 garlic cloves, crushed
1½ tablespoons extra virgin olive oil
125 ml (4 fl oz/½ cup) dry white wine

Preheat the oven to 180° C (350ºF /Gas 4).

Remove any fat from the cavity of the chicken. Rinse the chicken and pat dry inside and out with paper towels. Place the lemon halves and thyme sprigs inside the chicken and close the cavity with a small skewer or sturdy cocktail sticks. Tuck the wings under the bird and tie the legs securely with kitchen string.

Rub the chicken all over with the butter. Place in a roasting tin, breast side down, and bake for 45 minutes. Turn the chicken over, then arrange the potatoes around the chicken and bake for a further 20 minutes.

Add the brussels sprouts, chestnuts and bacon to the roasting tin, then sprinkle the vegetables with the garlic and drizzle with the olive oil. Bake for 30 minutes. Pour in the wine and bake for a further 10 minutes, or until the vegetables are tender and the chicken is cooked through.

Remove the chicken and transfer to a warm plate. Cover loosely with foil and leave to rest for 10 minutes. Turn the oven off but leave the vegetables in the oven to keep warm.

Carve the chicken and spoon the pan juices over. Serve with the chestnuts, bacon and the roasted vegetables.

✳ **Preparation time:** 15 minutes   ✳ **Cooking time:** 1 hour 45 minutes   ✳ **Serves:** 6

Preparation time: 30 minutes　Cooking time: 1 hour 30 minutes　Serves: 4

Root vegetable bake with crunchy cheesy almond crumbs

500 g (1 lb 2 oz) butternut pumpkin
(squash), peeled and cut into 4 cm
(1½ inch) chunks

600 g (1 lb 5 oz) sweet potato, peeled
and cut into 4 cm (1½ inch) chunks

400 g (14 oz) sebago potatoes, peeled
and cut into 4 cm (1½ inch) chunks

2 parsnips, peeled and cut into 4 cm
(1½ inch) chunks

3 red onions

60 ml (2 fl oz/¼ cup) olive oil

2 garlic cloves, chopped

1 small handful basil, plus extra,
to garnish

2 tablespoons tomato paste
(concentrated purée)

250 g (9 oz) cherry tomatoes

2 tablespoons cream

250 g (9 oz) Turkish bread, roughly
chopped

100 g (3½ oz/1 cup) grated parmesan
cheese

65 g (2½ oz/½ cup) grated gruyère
cheese

80 g (2¾ oz/½ cup) blanched almonds,
chopped

1 tablespoon oregano, chopped

Preheat the oven to 200°C (400°F/Gas 6).

Put the pumpkin, sweet potato, potato and parsnip in a large baking dish. Cut two of the onions into wedges 1.5 cm (⅝ inch) thick and add to the dish with 1 tablespoon of the olive oil. Toss to coat the vegetables, then season with sea salt and freshly ground black pepper. Roast for 1 hour, or until the vegetables are very tender.

Meanwhile, chop the remaining onion. Place in a food processor with the garlic, basil, tomato paste, tomatoes and cream, then blend until a coarse purée forms.

Put the bread in a bowl with the parmesan, gruyère, almonds, oregano and remaining oil. Mix together well.

Stir the puréed tomato mixture into the roasted vegetables until well coated, then scatter the breadcrumb mixture over the top. Bake for a further 30 minutes, or until the tomato mixture is bubbling and the topping is golden and crisp. Scatter with some more basil and serve.

Chicken, mushroom and tarragon pot pie

1 kg (2 lb 4 oz) chicken breast fillets,
  cut into 1 cm (½ inch) strips
60 g (2¼ oz) butter
4 shallots, thinly sliced
2 garlic cloves, crushed
500 g (1 lb 2 oz) button mushrooms,
  sliced
2 tablespoons plain (all-purpose) flour
125 ml (4 fl oz/½ cup) dry white wine
250 ml (9 fl oz/1 cup) cream
2 tablespoons chopped tarragon
2 teaspoons finely grated lemon rind

Topping
225 g (8 oz/1½ cups) self-raising flour
1½ teaspoons sea salt
40 g (1½ oz) butter, chilled and chopped
1 tablespoon snipped chives
1 large handful flat-leaf (Italian) parsley,
  chopped
185 ml (6 fl oz/¾ cup) milk

Preheat the oven to 170°C (325°F/Gas 3).

Season the chicken with sea salt and freshly ground black pepper. Heat half the butter in a flameproof casserole dish over medium–high heat until foaming. Add the chicken in batches and cook for 2 minutes on each side, or until seared and golden, removing each batch to a plate.

Melt the remaining butter in the dish. Sauté the shallot and garlic for 1 minute, then add the mushrooms and cook for a further 3–4 minutes, or until the mushrooms have softened.

Sprinkle the mushrooms with the flour and stir for 30 seconds, or until well blended. Slowly pour in the wine and stir until smooth. Cook, stirring, for 1–2 minutes, or until the liquid is thick. Pour in the cream and stir until just bubbling. Remove from the heat and add the chicken, tarragon and lemon rind. Set aside.

For the topping, sift the flour and salt into a bowl. Rub in the butter with your fingertips until the mixture resembles breadcrumbs. Stir in the herbs, then make a well in the centre. Using a flat-bladed knife, stir in 125 ml (4 fl oz/½ cup) of the milk to form a dough. Turn out onto a lightly floured surface and knead gently. Roll out to form a 20 x 35 cm (8 x 14 inch) rectangle and brush with some of the remaining milk. Roll the dough up from the long ends to form a tight roll. Cut into 1 cm (½ inch) slices.

Arrange the dough slices over the filling and brush generously with the remaining milk. Bake for 30–35 minutes, or until the filling is bubbling and the topping is golden and firm to the touch. Serve hot.

Preparation time: 25 minutes   **Cooking time:** 55 minutes   **Serves:** 6

Preparation time: 20 minutes   **Cooking time:** 1 hour 10 minutes   **Serves:** 4–6

Lamb, carrot and zucchini moussaka

1 tablespoon olive oil
1 onion, chopped
1 celery stalk, chopped
2 garlic cloves, chopped
500 g (1 lb 2 oz) lamb leg steaks, trimmed and cut into 2 cm (¾ inch) chunks
1 teaspoon dried oregano
1 carrot, cut into 1.5 cm (⅝ inch) chunks
1 zucchini (courgette), cut into 1.5 cm (⅝ inch) chunks
250 ml (9 fl oz/1 cup) tomato passata (puréed tomatoes)

Topping
2 eggs
250 g (9 oz/1 cup) plain yoghurt
75 g (2½ oz/½ cup) finely crumbled feta cheese
1 teaspoon cornflour (cornstarch)
½ teaspoon freshly ground nutmeg

Preheat the oven to 180°C (350°F/Gas 4).

Heat the olive oil in a 4 litre (140 fl oz/ 16 cup) flameproof roasting tin (measuring about 23 x 26 cm/9 x 10½ inches). Add the onion, celery and garlic and sauté over medium heat for 5 minutes, or until softened.

Meanwhile, put the lamb in a food processor and pulse briefly until finely chopped. Add to the roasting tin, with the oregano. Increase the heat to medium–high and sauté for 5 minutes, or until the lamb changes colour. Stir in the carrot and zucchini, then season well with sea salt and freshly ground black pepper.

Stir in the passata and bring the mixture to a simmer. Cover, transfer to the oven and bake for 40 minutes, or until the lamb is tender and the sauce is thick.

For the topping, whisk the ingredients in a bowl until smooth. Carefully pour over the lamb mixture, spreading it to cover evenly. Bake, uncovered, for a further 15 minutes, or until the topping is just set.

Remove from the oven and allow to stand for 5 minutes to cool slightly before serving.

If you're in a hurry, you could chop the vegetables in a food processor, using the pulse button. Instead of the lamb leg steaks, you can also use minced (ground) lamb in this recipe.

Baked stuffed meatloaf

The meatloaf mixture can be made and shaped the night before; cover and refrigerate it until you are ready to cook.

60 ml (2 fl oz/¼ cup) olive oil
600 g (1 lb 5 oz) minced (ground) beef
600 g (1 lb 5 oz) minced (ground) pork
1 onion, very finely chopped
2 garlic cloves, crushed
2 tablespoons chopped marjoram
  (or use oregano)
2 eggs, lightly beaten
120 g (4¼ oz/1½ cups) fresh
  breadcrumbs
100 g (3½ oz) sliced salami, chopped
100 g (3½ oz) sharp cheddar cheese,
  cut into 1 cm (½ inch) cubes
4 tinned artichoke hearts, drained
  and quartered
3 red onions, thinly sliced
350 g (12 oz) roasting potatoes,
  scrubbed and cut into wedges
1 tablespoon balsamic vinegar

Preheat the oven to 180°C (350°F/Gas 4). Drizzle 2 tablespoons of the olive oil over the base of a large baking dish.

Put the beef, pork, onion, garlic, marjoram, eggs and breadcrumbs in a bowl. Season well with sea salt and freshly ground black pepper and mix using clean hands until well combined. Turn the mixture out onto a large clean board. Using damp hands, flatten the meat to a rectangle about 2.5 cm (1 inch) thick. Arrange the salami, cheese and artichokes down the centre of the meat. Gently mould the meat around the filling, tucking the ends in to enclose the filling and to form an oblong-shaped meatloaf.

Place the baking dish in the hot oven for 5–10 minutes, or until very hot. Carefully transfer the meatloaf to the centre of the dish. Bake for 20 minutes.

Arrange the onion and potato around the meatloaf, drizzle with the vinegar and remaining olive oil and bake for another 40 minutes. Cover the dish loosely with foil, then bake for a final 20 minutes, or until the meat is cooked through and the vegetables are very tender.

Remove the meatloaf from the oven. Leave the foil on and allow the meatloaf to stand in a warm place for 10–15 minutes before slicing and serving with the onion and potato.

Preparation time: 15 minutes   **Cooking time:** 25 minutes   **Serves:** 4–6

Lamb steaks baked with tomato, lentils, mint and feta

1½ tablespoons olive oil

6 boneless lamb leg steaks (about 800 g/ 1 lb 12 oz in total)

1 red onion, sliced into thin rings

2 garlic cloves, crushed

400 g (14 oz) tin chopped tomatoes

400 g (14 oz) tin lentils, rinsed and drained

1 small handful small mint leaves

80 g (2¾ oz/½ cup) pitted kalamata olives

100 g (3½ oz/⅔ cup) crumbled feta cheese

Preheat the oven to 220°C (425°F/Gas 7).

Place a large baking dish in the oven to heat for 5 minutes.

Using a little of the olive oil, brush the lamb on both sides and arrange in a single layer in the hot baking dish. Scatter the onion over the top and bake for 10 minutes.

Put the remaining oil in a bowl with the garlic, tomatoes, lentils and half the mint. Season to taste with sea salt and freshly ground black pepper and mix together well. Spoon the mixture over the lamb and bake for 10 minutes.

Scatter the olives, feta and remaining mint over the lamb and serve.

Beef steaks, lamb cutlets or veal chops could also be used here instead of the lamb steaks, although the cooking time may need to be adjusted slightly depending on the thickness of the cut. You can also vary the herbs — use basil, oregano or even thyme instead of the mint.

Pork and chorizo pie

750 g (1 lb 10 oz) pork neck,
 trimmed and cut into 3 cm (1¼ inch)
 chunks
plain (all-purpose) flour, for dusting
2 tablespoons olive oil
2 mild chorizo sausages, cut into
 1 cm (½ inch) chunks
1 large onion, chopped
2 garlic cloves, crushed
1 teaspoon ground coriander
1 teaspoon ground cumin
¼ teaspoon ground cinnamon
400 g (14 oz) tin chopped tomatoes
185 ml (6 fl oz/¾ cup) beef stock
400 g (14 oz) tin chickpeas, rinsed
 and drained
1 small handful coriander (cilantro)
 leaves

Pastry
110 g (3¾ oz/¾ cup) self-raising flour
35 g (1¼ oz/¼ cup) polenta, plus extra,
 for sprinkling
a pinch of chilli flakes
50 g (1¾ oz) butter, chilled and chopped
1 egg, lightly beaten
milk, for glazing

Preheat the oven to 180°C (350°F/Gas 4).

Dust the pork in the flour, shaking off any excess. Heat half the olive oil in a 4 litre (140 fl oz/16 cup) flameproof casserole dish over medium–high heat. Cook the pork and chorizo in batches for 5–6 minutes, or until lightly browned all over, turning often. Remove each batch to a bowl using a slotted spoon.

Heat the remaining oil in the dish. Reduce the heat to medium and sauté the onion and garlic for 2–3 minutes, or until starting to brown. Add the ground spices and stir until fragrant. Stir in the tomatoes, stock and chickpeas, then add the pork, chorizo and any pan juices and mix well. Bring to the boil over high heat, then cover, transfer to the oven and bake for 45 minutes.

Remove the lid and bake for a further 20 minutes, or until the pork is tender and the sauce has thickened. Remove from the oven, stir in the coriander and season with sea salt and freshly ground black pepper. Allow to cool slightly while making the pastry.

For the pastry, put the flour, polenta and chilli flakes in a large bowl with a pinch of salt. Rub in the butter using your fingertips until the mixture resembles fine breadcrumbs. Make a well in the centre, add the egg and stir using a flat-bladed knife until the mixture comes together. Turn out onto a lightly floured surface and knead lightly until just smooth. Roll the pastry out so it is slightly larger than the casserole dish, then carefully place it over the top of the dish. Brush lightly with milk and sprinkle with a little extra polenta.

Bake for 30–35 minutes, or until the pastry is golden and the pork is heated through.

Preparation time: 40 minutes   **Cooking time:** 2 hours   **Serves:** 4

INDEX

Published in 2010 by Murdoch Books Pty Limited

Murdoch Books Australia
Pier 8/9
23 Hickson Road
Millers Point NSW 2000
Phone: +61 (0) 2 8220 2000
Fax: +61 (0) 2 8220 2558
www.murdochbooks.com.au

Murdoch Books UK Limited
Erico House, 6th Floor
93–99 Upper Richmond Road
Putney, London SW15 2TG
Phone: +44 (0) 20 8785 5995
Fax: +44 (0) 20 8785 5985
www.murdochbooks.co.uk

Publishing director: Kay Scarlett
Project editor: Kristin Buesing
Food editor: Leanne Kitchen
Copy editor: Katri Hilden
Cover concept: Yolande Gray
Design concept: Emilia Toia
Photographer: Stuart Scott
Stylist: Sarah O'Brien
Food preparation: Peta Dent, Andrew De Sousa, Abi Ulgiati
Recipes developed by Peta Dent, Michelle Earl, Heidi Flett, Fiona Hammond, Leanne Kitchen, Kathy Knudsen, Barbara Lowery, Kim Meredith, Angela Tregonning and the Murdoch Books test kitchen.

National Library of Australia Cataloguing-in-Publication
Title: One-pot wonders.
ISBN: 9781741964431 (pbk.)
Series: My kitchen series
Notes: Includes index.
Subjects: One-dish meals.
             Cookery.
Dewey Number: 641.82

A catalogue record for this book is available from the British Library.

PRINTED IN CHINA.

IMPORTANT: Those who might be at risk from the effects of salmonella poisoning (the elderly, pregnant women, young children and those suffering from immune deficiency diseases) should consult their doctor with any concerns about eating raw eggs.

OVEN GUIDE: You may find cooking times vary depending on the oven you are using. For fan-forced ovens, as a general rule, set the oven temperature to 20°C (35°F) lower than indicated in the recipe.

The **My Kitchen** series is packed with sensational flavours, simple methods and vibrant photographs. What's more, these easy, inexpensive and well-tested recipes use only commonly available ingredients and fresh seasonal produce. And because cooking should be a joy, there's a little bit of magic in these recipes too!

One-Pot Wonders is the perfect book for busy cooks who detest washing up. From the great cuisines of the world, we've handpicked a tempting smorgasbord of marvellous recipes that let you cook up a storm — in just one pot! Whether you're craving a creamy risotto or a comforting bake, you'll find our recipes are low on effort but big on effect, and perfect for any occasion.

£12.99

ISBN 978-1741964431

9 781741 964431

MURDOCH BOOKS